KV-578-838

**New Directions for
Teaching and Learning**

Marilla D. Svinicki
Catherine M. Wehlburg
Co-Editors-in-Chief

Pathways to the Profession of Educational Development

Jeanette McDonald
Denise Stockley
Editors

Number 122 • Summer 2010
Jossey-Bass
San Francisco

PATHWAYS TO THE PROFESSION OF EDUCATIONAL DEVELOPMENT
Jeanette McDonald, Denise Stockley (eds.)
New Directions for Teaching and Learning, no. 122
Marilla D. Svinicki, Catherine M. Wehlburg, Co-Editors-in-Chief

Microfilm copies of issues and articles are available in 16mm and 35mm, as well as microfiche in 105mm, through University Microfilms, Inc., 300 North Zeeb Road, Ann Arbor, MI 48106-1346.

NEW DIRECTIONS FOR TEACHING AND LEARNING (ISSN 0271-0633, electronic ISSN 1536-0768) is part of The Jossey-Bass Higher and Adult Education Series and is published quarterly by Wiley Subscription Services, Inc., A Wiley Company, at Jossey-Bass, 989 Market Street, San Francisco, CA 94103-1741. Periodicals postage paid at San Francisco, CA, and at additional mailing offices. POSTMASTER: Send address changes to New Directions for Teaching and Learning, Jossey-Bass, 989 Market Street, San Francisco, CA 94103-1741.

New Directions for Teaching and Learning is indexed in CIJE: Current Index to Journals in Education (ERIC), Contents Pages in Education (T&F), Current Abstracts (EBSCO), Educational Research Abstracts Online (T&F), ERIC Database (Education Resources Information Center), Higher Education Abstracts (Claremont Graduate University), and SCOPUS (Elsevier).

SUBSCRIPTIONS cost $98 for individuals and $267 for institutions, agencies, and libraries in the United States. Prices subject to change.

EDITORIAL CORRESPONDENCE should be sent to the co-editor-in-chief, Marilla D. Svinicki, Department of Educational Psychology, University of Texas at Austin, One University Station, D5800, Austin, TX 78712.

www.josseybass.com

CONTENTS

FROM THE SERIES EDITORS

About This Publication

Since 1980, *New Directions for Teaching and Learning (NDTL)* has brought a unique blend of theory, research, and practice to leaders in postsecondary education. *NDTL* sourcebooks strive not only for solid substance but also for timeliness, compactness, and accessibility.

The series has four goals: to inform readers about current and future directions in teaching and learning in postsecondary education, to illuminate the context that shapes these new directions, to illustrate these new directions through examples from real settings, and to propose ways in which these new directions can be incorporated into still other settings.

This publication reflects the view that teaching deserves respect as a high form of scholarship. We believe that significant scholarship is conducted both by researchers who report results of empirical investigations and by practitioners who share disciplinary reflections about teaching. Contributors to *NDTL* approach questions of teaching and learning as seriously as they approach substantive questions in their own disciplines, and they deal with pedagogical issues as well as the intellectual and social context in which these issues arise. Authors deal on the one hand with theory and research and on the other with practice, and they translate from research and theory to practice and back again.

About This Volume

Educational development is an important area of research, study, and practice in higher education. Over the last several decades, this area has moved from a relatively individualistic approach to being a collaborative and scholarly field that has broad impact on teaching and learning. This volume, specifically, provides insight on how individuals enter and operate within the field of educational development.

Marilla D. Svinicki
Catherine M. Wehlburg
Co-Editors-in-Chief

MARILLA D. SVINICKI is the director of the Center for Teaching Effectiveness at the University of Texas at Austin.

CATHERINE M. WEHLBURG is the assistant provost for Institutional Effectiveness at Texas Christian University.

FOREWORD

Plus Ça Change . . . Educational Development Past and Future

Christopher Knapper

The chapters in this volume focus on the origins and evolution of educational development over the past fifty years, examining the movement's growth and impact, and suggesting likely future directions. As the editors point out in their introduction, educational development as we know it today began in the early 1960s—coincidentally, just as I was starting my own academic career. The Canadian Association of University Teachers (CAUT) was one of a number of national organizations concerned with the lack of professional preparation of faculty for their different roles, especially teaching, and I became chair of a CAUT committee charged with making recommendations on such matters. (Out of this committee, among other things, came the concept of the teaching portfolio for documenting and reflecting on teaching achievements.)

In 1973, I spent a sabbatical leave making a more systematic study of various initiatives in several parts of the world to enhance the quality of university teaching and train faculty for their teaching responsibilities. I visited several dozen institutions in Britain and Europe, North America, Australia, New Zealand, and a few places in between. Readers may be surprised to know (as I was) that there was already a small teaching and learning center at the University of the South Pacific in tiny Fiji. In the course of the trip, I met many remarkable individuals, among them the indomitable Barbara Falk from the University of Melbourne, identified in Jeanette McDonald and Denise Stockley's introductory notes as the first professional educational developer.

NEW DIRECTIONS FOR TEACHING AND LEARNING, no. 122, Summer 2010 © Wiley Periodicals, Inc.
Published online in Wiley InterScience (www.interscience.wiley.com) • DOI: 10.1002/tl.392

As this volume makes clear, the impetus for better preparation of faculty and enhancement of teaching was almost certainly the rapid expansion of universities, beginning in the 1960s, and the exponential rise in the number of students attending college, many from nontraditional backgrounds. This in turn required more postsecondary teachers and recruitment of many (myself included) who would probably never have found a position in the traditional university.

And what of the educational developers? (The term was not even used at that time.) What was their background and motivation? How did they go about their work? How did they judge the effectiveness of their programs? A few were psychologists with a research interest in teaching and learning. A few others had a background in education, and the rest came from a range of disciplines. In rank, they were likely to be more senior than junior, and often appointed to an additional position to set up a teaching and learning center on a trial basis. A few of the units were established on a permanent footing with a senior tenured professor as director (for example, the University Teaching and Research Centre at Victoria University, Wellington, New Zealand). Others were supported by "soft money" (from foundations), sometimes very generously, but disappeared once the grants had been exhausted. (A famous example is the Clinic to Improve University Teaching at the University of Massachusetts.)

What has changed in educational development? What seems still the same? I have worked in the field now for thirty-five years, and the most obvious change is the growth of educational development worldwide, in both developed and developing countries—though there are some puzzling gaps, such as the general indifference to improving teaching in Southern and Eastern Europe. The units I visited in 1973–74 all had the common goal of improving teaching (and, implicitly, enriching student learning), but their approaches often differed substantially. Some, like the Clinic to Improve University Teaching, as the name suggests, had a remedial philosophy based on individual consultation and counseling. Others, especially in Britain, placed great emphasis on induction courses for faculty (especially new appointees) that focused on basic principles and practices of effective teaching. A number of centers in North America were heavily involved in student evaluation of teaching, and others made great use of mentoring and peer consultation.

Chapters in the present volume show that, if anything, contemporary educational development is perhaps more homogeneous than it was forty years ago, probably because of greatly increased communication among developers internationally and sharing of good practice. Hence almost all centers offer a program of workshops and short courses, and many run more comprehensive certificate programs on teaching and learning in higher education for faculty and graduate students. Almost all centers have extensive Web sites to make available information about university teaching. Most offer a specialized resource library, coordinate teaching awards, and provide individual consultation on teaching problems; and many have small grants programs for teaching-related research and development projects. In North America, where almost all graduate students do some teaching, practically every center offers special programs for teaching assistants. Increasingly, centers are also concerned with curriculum development and, especially in Europe and Australia, involve themselves with quality assurance issues as they relate to teaching and learning.

Given this commonality, we might assume that educational development is now established on a firm footing worldwide, is accepted as a permanent and worthwhile part of the academy, and is largely in agreement on its goals and activities. However, the pages of this sourcebook indicate that there remains quite a number of unresolved issues relating to educational development practice.

A major issue—indeed, it is part of the title of this volume—is the question of the *professionalization of educational development*. Many developers have been advocates for the professionalization of university teaching, and it seems plausible that educational development itself might move toward becoming a profession. At the moment there is no commonly recognized initial training or qualification for educational developers, although in Britain the Staff and Educational Development Association has for some years offered an accreditation program for its members (described in the chapter by Kym Fraser, David Gosling, and Mary Deane Sorcinelli). Professionalization would of course require some agreement on a conceptual basis of the field. For example, is our main focus on improving teaching, or should faculty development also extend to research and administrative roles (as originally envisaged by the CAUT)? Should developers themselves be established academics, for example doing research, teaching undergraduates, serving on faculty committees, and so on? What theories of teaching and learning inform the approach we take to our work? What theories of development and change underpin our programs (an issue raised in the chapter by Debra Dawson, Joy Mighty, and Judy Britnell)? Is educational development best provided at an institutional level, or should it be largely discipline-based and offered by developers who have research and teaching expertise in the relevant department, as discussed in the chapter by Lynn Taylor?

A second and related theme that emerges in these pages relates to the *goals, context, and status* of educational development. Despite the gains made over the last forty years, in many institutions educational development is still a marginal activity (as discussed in the chapters by Karron Lewis and Jeanette McDonald). Relatively few developers have academic tenure, and even fewer have professorial rank. Although it is increasingly common for centers to undertake some research on their practice, much of the seminal research that informs our field is done outside educational development centers.

NEW DIRECTIONS FOR TEACHING AND LEARNING • DOI: 10.1002/tl

What is the appropriate skill set for a developer? Clearly, knowledge of university teaching and learning pedagogy is required, but the day-to-day work of a developer also requires skills in communication, human relations, program development, and organization—abilities more commonly taught in business school than in most traditional academic departments. How does our work relate to other ancillary activities, such as the university library, student services, and the computer center? A particularly intriguing question concerns the link between educational development and educational technology, where there has always been a somewhat uneasy relationship, in part because many technologies are quite ephemeral and resource-intensive.

Even more important is the question of whom educational developers serve: faculty? students? the university administration? This issue can be especially problematic in an institutional context where a center is given major responsibility for quality assurance processes or course evaluation. To what extent should the work of developers reflect institutional and societal values, and what should be the stance of developers in challenging such values, if appropriate (what Gosling in his chapter intriguingly refers to as the "morality" of educational development)? How, as Sorcinelli and Ann Austin discuss, should developers be evaluated and rewarded, and how will this differ for those staff and faculty appointments?

The last set of issues concerns the *impact and effectiveness* of educational development, which at a time of budgetary constraints has caused great soul searching among practitioners worldwide. In fact, there is a small but growing body of evidence (discussed in the chapter by Carolyn Hoessler, Britnell, and Stockley) that faculty participation in educational development activities (from seeking consultation on a teaching problem to taking an induction course) does enhance both professors' teaching as well as their students' learning. But developers are always being challenged to justify their existence with hard data in a manner that would be uncommon for, say, the physics or history department.

These, then, are some of the issues and dilemmas facing educational developers in the next fifty years, and discussed in the chapters that follow. Our community is both reflective and imaginative, and I have no doubt we will rise to the challenge. We have achieved a great deal in improving instructional effectiveness in the first five decades of our existence, but there is a great deal more work to be done to ensure that teaching remains central to our work as academics, and that universities and colleges remain places where learning is preeminent.

CHRISTOPHER KNAPPER is an international consultant on educational development. He is Professor Emeritus, Psychology, at Queen's University, Canada. He has been a professional academic developer for 30 years, and founded two of

Canada's major instructional development centres, the first at the University of Waterloo in 1977, and later at Queen's University. He also helped to found Canada's national organization for educational development, the Society for Teaching and Learning in Higher Education (STLHE), of which he served as first president from 1984–88. In 2002 STLHE created the "Christopher Knapper Lifetime Achievement Award" in his name.

NEW DIRECTIONS FOR TEACHING AND LEARNING • DOI: 10.1002/tl

Editors' Notes

Educational development as a field of practice is a relatively new phenomenon within the postsecondary landscape. Our history began in Australia with the University Teaching Project, set up by Barbara Falk in 1961, though her unit was first established in 1958 (Lee, Manathunga, and Kandlbinder, 2008), and in the United States with the first teaching and learning center founded in 1962 (Ouellett, 2010). During this fifty-year history, educational development and the developer role have moved from the periphery to the mainstream of higher education, becoming more visible and active at the local, national, and international levels. The profile and legitimacy of educational development as a profession have increased over the years with more and more individuals moving into this field (Sorcinelli, Austin, Eddy, and Beach, 2006). However, there is no prescribed entry point or career progression to guide access to and movement within the field of educational development. It is critical that we document the pathways for individuals on the periphery, those on the outside of the field, as well as newcomers and seasoned educational developers to impart a sense of the possibilities that a career in educational development will allow. By doing so, we add to the literature on educational development and the more recent critical perspective of development/developer practice, position, and place.

Our work stems from a think tank that was held in Ottawa, Canada, in June 2007, which was tasked with developing an international research agenda of the varying paths to our field (McDonald and Stockley, 2008). This think tank was funded through the Social Sciences and Humanities Research Council of Canada and was the first funded research in Canada to explore educational development as a profession. During the three years since this think tank, the authors have published, presented, and applied for grants in order to seed a pathways agenda. This volume is a composite of our work and offers a lens on our efforts to document and reflect on pathways to and within the profession of educational development as the field and our scope of practice continue to evolve in response to internal and external drivers.

This volume is divided into three sections: context, practice, and reflections. Each chapter adds to an evolving understanding of what constitutes educational development. Within the context section, Karron Lewis begins the volume with a cross-cultural overview of the field of educational development from our foundations to the present time. The second chapter, by Mary Deane Sorcinelli and Ann Austin, draws on the experiences of individuals within our field and takes a snapshot of a dataset of close to five hundred educational developers, describing the structures they operate within and the influences that helped set their pathways. In the third chapter, Jeanette McDonald maps three entry points into the field and the associated contexts shaping these pathways, based on interview data with Canadian educational developers at various stages in their career (early, middle, and late).

The second section focuses on the practice of educational development. Kym Fraser, David Gosling, and Mary Deane Sorcinelli highlight several models and approaches within educational development, recognizing that within our field there is no one-size-fits-all for our multifaceted enterprise. Delving deeper into our expanding role within the disciplines, Lynn Taylor explores the place of disciplinary knowledge and culture in Chapter Five, and how an understanding of "knowing in" the disciplines aids the educational developer in collaboration with disciplinary colleagues. The final chapter in this section, by Debra Dawson, Joy Mighty, and Judy Britnell, highlights how our traditional developer roles and scope of practice are broadening to include other responsibilities, in this case that of change agent.

The final section shares reflections through a critical lens of how we operate within our field. In Chapter Seven, Carolyn Hoessler, Judy Britnell, and Denise Stockley recommend a scholarly approach to determine the impact of individual centers and developers on the changing culture of teaching and learning within the institution. From there, David Gosling explores and debates the values associated with educational development through the lens of the individual, center, institution, professional association, and wider community. The final chapter in this volume, by Joy Mighty, Mathew Ouellett, and Christine Stanley, examines the voices typically unheard within educational development and the consequences that come with their exclusion.

References

Lee, A., Manathunga, C., and Kandlbinder, P.A. (eds.). *Making a Place: An Oral History of Academic Development in Australia.* Milperra, N.S.W.: Higher Education Research and Development Society of Australasia, 2008.

McDonald, J., and Stockley, D. "Pathways to the Profession of Educational Development: An International Perspective." *International Journal for Academic Development,* 2008, *13*(3), 213–218.

Ouellett, M. L. Overview of Faculty Development: History and Choices. In K. J. Gillespie, D. L. Robertson, and Associates (eds.). *A Guide to Faculty Development* (2nd ed). San Francisco: Jossey Bass, 2010.

Sorcinelli, M. D., Austin, A. E., Eddy, P. L., and Beach, A. L. *Creating the Future of Faculty Development: Learning from the Past, Understanding the Present*. Bolton, Mass.: Anker, 2006.

Jeanette McDonald
Denise Stockley
Editors

JEANETTE MCDONALD *has worked in educational development for more than ten years, first at the University of Guelph and now at Wilfrid Laurier University. Currently she is the manager of educational development in the Office of Teaching Support Services. She is the co-leader of the Pathways Initiative.*

DENISE STOCKLEY *joined the Center for Teaching and Learning at Queen's University in 2001. She is the associate director and also an associate professor of education. She is the co-leader of the Pathways Initiative.*

SECTION ONE

Context

1

People are drawn to the field of improving teaching and learning in higher education from a variety of disciplines and backgrounds, but before we look at these "pathways," we need to delve into the history, international variations, and similarities of the field of faculty/educational/academic development to provide a context for what has happened to make this field important to the vitality of teaching and learning in higher education all over the world.

Pathways Toward Improving Teaching and Learning in Higher Education: International Context and Background

Karron G. Lewis

Improving teaching and learning in higher education became an important international endeavor in the 1960s and 1970s, corresponding to an influx of students coming in greater numbers than ever seen before, from a broader range of backgrounds, and with diverse expectations for attending colleges and universities. These same students were also more politically mindful and active as they began to demand "the right to exercise some control over the quality of their undergraduate learning experience, by such means as evaluating their teachers' performance in the classroom" (Sorcinelli, Austin, Eddy, and Beach, 2006, p. 2). Sit-ins and student protests over "irrelevant courses and uninspired teaching" (Graff and Simpson, 1994, p. 168) challenged postsecondary institutions to modify traditional ways of teaching. No longer was a thorough knowledge of the subject matter enough to teach effectively in higher education. Concurrently, economic conditions made it difficult for colleges and universities to hire unlimited numbers of faculty or to "buy" sought-after faculty from other institutions. Thus faculty members stayed in one place longer, increasingly relying on their institution to support their professional and personal growth (Lewis, 1996).

Fortunately institutional champions of teaching and learning (teachers, researchers, administrators, technicians) saw the need for this kind of support on their campuses:

> Many large universities [already] had established offices to provide techno-
> logical support for instruction, . . . [such that] by the 1960s it was common
> to find former audiovisual aid centers engaged in the promotion of instruc-
> tional design concepts as the basis for technical assistance ranging from indi-
> vidualized self-paced learning to multi-media presentations [North and
> Scholl, 1979, p. 10].

In the United States, private foundations such as Ford and Andrew
Mellon began to make institutional grants to encourage efforts to enhance
learning. In 1973, the American Association for Higher Education (AAHE)
featured sessions on "instructional development as practiced at Syracuse
University, large-scale media productions as developed at SUNY-Albany,
and small-scale feedback experiments supported by the Kellogg Foundation" (North and Scholl, 1979, p. 10). At the same time, regional groups
started to come together to share expertise and focus institutional attention
on the quality of teaching (North and Scholl, 1979). Although AAHE no
longer exists, this organization constituted an early venue for discussions
of faculty development and enhancing teaching and learning in higher
education on the part of college and university administrators—the very
people who enact change at their institutions.

The International Terminology of Improving Teaching and Learning

Labels and descriptions of efforts to improve teaching and learning in
higher education vary across countries, reflecting regional understandings
of development work, unit program offerings, and center positioning
within organizational structures. In the United States, for example, the field
is known as "faculty development," and units housing development programs are known by a variety of names, among them Teaching and Learning
Center, Center for Instructional Development and Research, Center for
Teaching Excellence, and Faculty and Graduate Student Instructors Development Center. In the United Kingdom and Canada, the field is known as
"educational development," with center titles going by the same name or
reflective of the programs offered or the area in which the units are housed
within a larger umbrella structure—for example, Educational Development
and Support Service, Instructional Development Center, Teaching Support
Services, and Center for University Teaching and Learning. In Australia
and New Zealand, the field is known as "academic development" or "academic staff development." Center titles here likewise reflect their services
and include, for example, Center for Teaching and Learning, Professional
Development Center, and Higher Education Development Center, and so
forth.

Today, teaching and learning development units are forming all over the world, and their proximity to one of the countries mentioned here frequently seems to determine the terminology used. For consistency, the term *faculty development* is used in the remainder of this chapter.

Program Areas of Teaching and Learning Development

The range and type of programs and services offered by development units are shaped by a number of factors, not the least of which are the needs and interests of faculty and academic staff. An expansion of this theme can be found in Sorcinelli and Austin's chapter in this volume, which outlines the level of impact of several such factors. The educational literature consistently reports on the signature offerings of teaching and learning centers even though their focus and audience may vary according to institutional and external trends and initiatives. They include, for example, individual and group consultations; universitywide and department-based orientations, workshops, intensive programs, and technical assistance; research on the evaluation of teaching; teaching and innovation grants and awards; mentoring and support services; and resource libraries and publications (Justice, 1979; Sorcinelli, Austin, Eddy, and Beach, 2006; Wright and O'Neil, 1995).

Although there is similarity in center activities around the world, how they are delivered can vary substantially. To thrive, programs must reflect the culture of their institution. Concerning this, Hicks (1999) outlines four primary models for the "delivery of academic [faculty] development." The *central model* is the most prevalent or traditional model practiced worldwide. It consists of a strong central unit that has responsibility for providing faculty development programs for the entire campus, with few programs if any geared for particular departments. The *dispersed model* typically focuses at the departmental level and "is likely to be accompanied by policy to encourage such activity within the institution" (1999, p. 47). Unfortunately, some institutions use this model to argue that a central unit is not necessary and that responsibility for faculty development can be moved to departments alone. The *mixed model* offers the best of both worlds: central generic programs and discipline-specific offerings at the local level. This can, however, result in a lack of program coordination and possible duplication of effort. Lastly, the *integrated model* enables incorporation of elements from the mixed model, yielding a more "holistic approach" (Brew and Boud, 1996, p. 17). This model is more difficult to establish, but it is seen as "the most robust and effective, ensuring an ongoing central and local involvement in academic development" (Hicks, 1999, p. 48). Refer to Fraser, Gosling, and Sorcinelli's chapter for an in-depth overview of evolving models of faculty development at the individual, institutional, and sector levels.

NEW DIRECTIONS FOR TEACHING AND LEARNING • DOI: 10.1002/tl

Funding for Faculty Development Centers

In some countries, faculty development programs are mandated or strongly encouraged by the government. In Sweden, for example, "staff [faculty] development, more than general educational development, is institutionalized to a high degree due to the central system and provision of funds for training university teachers" (Moses, 1987, p. 465). In 1976, Swedish institutions were required by law to offer a five-day induction program for all staff, which was compulsory for new staff. In 2001, the Swedish National Committee of Inquiry into the Renewal of Learning and Teaching in Higher Education published a report indicating that it was the "responsibility of the individual teacher, the department and the institution to take initiatives that will develop learning and teaching" (Roxå and Mårtensson, 2008, p. 155). The following year, national legislation passed requiring "all new academic staff, in order to get tenure academic positions, to participate in ten weeks of pedagogical courses" (p. 156). Australia and the United Kingdom likewise have mandated development of teaching and learning units or provided incentive funding for the development of such centers.

In 1997, a significant event affecting the future of faculty development in the United Kingdom was the report of the National Committee of Inquiry into Higher Education, known as the Dearing Report. In it,

> Dearing suggested that teachers in higher education need professional development both at the outset of their careers and thereafter. The report recommended that an institute be created which would have among its goals the accreditation of courses for lecturers preparing to teach in higher education and the promotion of Continuous Professional Development [as cited by Gosling, 2001, p. 76].

Consequently, in 2005 the government launched a major initiative to reward and promote excellence in teaching by establishing and funding seventy-four Centers for Excellence in Teaching and Learning (CELT). In addition to these general centers, twenty-four subject-specific centers—the Learning and Teaching Support Network—were established. Their formation enabled collaboration between developers at all centers when working with faculty in specific fields.

In the United States, faculty development centers were often started with grants from private foundations or public agencies (examples are the Lilly Endowment, National Science Foundation, and Fund for the Improvement of Postsecondary Education). The grants typically lasted between three and five years, at which time the institution was responsible for providing base funding. In most cases, these centers met with success. Today the majority of faculty development units in the United States are funded through university budgets or endowments.

NEW DIRECTIONS FOR TEACHING AND LEARNING • DOI: 10.1002/tl

Timelines for Center Formation

Many countries can trace the formation of one or more early faculty development centers, programs, or committees to the 1960s. The first faculty development center in the United States was the Center for Research on Learning and Teaching at the University of Michigan–Ann Arbor, founded in 1962 (Ouellett, 2010). Even though there were fewer than fifty faculty development programs in the United States at the end of the decade (Sullivan, 1983), by 1975 60 percent of all institutions indicated they had organized faculty development programs (Centra, 1976). More specifically, a 1986 survey found that 44 percent of all four-year institutions (including large and small, private and public) had faculty development programs, while in 1995 Crawley found that 64 percent of the 104 research universities (as classified by the Carnegie Foundation for the Advancement of Teaching) had an individual designated as coordinator or director of a faculty or instructional development program or unit. Today, in the United States there are more and more faculty development programs being formed and many more new individuals entering the field. This is evidenced by the work of Sorcinelli and her colleagues, and as well at the 2008 and 2009 Professional and Organizational Development Network's New Developers Pre-Conference Workshop at which the seventy-five attendees each year indicated having zero to three years of experience and were in new programs.

In the United Kingdom, the first educational development unit was founded at Surrey in 1967 (Gosling, 2006). By 1990, there were nineteen such units, and by the end of 2005 seventy-five. In some instances, smaller institutions had a teaching and learning committee, rather than an organized educational development unit through which educational and instructional activities and programs were coordinated. Incentives from the Higher Education Funding Council for England encouraged institutions to show how their units had achieved excellence and how they would develop further to disseminate good practice both within and beyond their institutions. Funding was also given to develop new units and programs. Thus there was a proliferation of new centers in a short period of time (Gosling and Hannan, 2007).

In Australia, "the call for research into teaching methods and into causes for wastage and high failure rates made by committees had led a few universities by the mid-sixties to establish, by various names, academic or educational development units with their primary function the improvement of teaching" (Moses, 1987, p. 454). In some cases, student requests for academic development units led to their establishment in a number of universities: "The Universities Commission in its Fifth Report in May 1972 accepted students' assertion that [academic development] units contributed to improved teaching and recommended that all universities establish one" (p. 454). There are currently twenty-five institutions

NEW DIRECTIONS FOR TEACHING AND LEARNING • DOI: 10.1002/tl

in Australia, six in New Zealand, and one in Fiji that have academic development units.

Center Closures and the Ramifications

At a time when many new teaching and learning units are opening their doors, others are closing down. Most of the closures can be attributed to budget cuts, changes in administration, lack of understanding of the benefits of faculty development, or an ambivalent commitment to excellence in teaching. As public postsecondary institutions in the United States are receiving less and less financial support from their state legislatures, colleges and universities are looking for places where expenses can be cut. Constance E. Cook, director of the University of Michigan teaching center, says, "As budgets tighten, teaching centers need to strengthen their ties with other university offices and make sure that administrators see that the various offices are working in harmony" (Glenn, 2009). The most notable closure in the United States was the Teaching and Learning Center at the University of Nebraska, Lincoln, in the spring of 2002. This center was established in 1970 and was the second oldest center in the country; it was the model for many centers that were formed between 1970 and 2002. The cut saved the university about $400,000 a year (Bartlett, 2002). When asked where the faculty who desired feedback on their teaching would go, administration responded "their own departments." Unfortunately, very few departments wish to or are able to supply all or even most of the services the center originally offered, particularly the same level of confidentiality and trust of a neutral third party. The University of Nebraska center was the most visible center to be closed, but there have been numerous others, in the United States and the United Kingdom (Gosling, 2009). This reality speaks to the importance of situating our work within the heart of the institution and higher education overall. Other chapters in this book give examples of how to do this and the cautions that come with them.

National Teaching and Learning Organizations

North and Scholl (1979) reported that by 1973 interest in faculty development was fairly widespread, but many who were working alone on their campus felt a need for support from colleagues in this new endeavor. In time, regional groups began to form, furnishing a space to share expertise and organize conferences to bring institutional attention to the quality of instruction in higher education. In 1975, approximately 150 delegates attending the annual conference of the American Association of Higher Education came together to discuss a proposed national organization. From this the Professional and Organizational Development Network in Higher Education (POD Network) was born (North and Scholl, 1979). As teaching and learning in higher education emerged in other countries, additional national organizations were formed.

A milestone in international cooperation took place in 1993 when Graham Gibbs from England convened a meeting of the presidents of existing national faculty development organizations to share knowledge and strategies being used in various countries and to lend assistance to faculty development organizations just getting started. From this, the International Consortium for Educational Development (ICED) emerged (http://www.osds.uwa.edu.au/iced, retrieved January 5, 2010). The consortium has since hosted seven conferences, held every two years, with attendance of 200-plus participants reported at the most recent meeting in 2008. The organizations listed here, with their year of inception if known, are currently members of the International Consortium for Educational Development:

- Australasia: Higher Education Research and Development Society of Australasia (HERDSA), 1997
- Belgium: Contact Group for Higher Education (CgHO)
- Canada: The Society for Teaching and Learning in Higher Education (STLHE), 1981
- Croatia: Society for Development of Higher Education (UNIVERSITAS), 2000
- Denmark: Dansk Universitetspædagogisk Netværk (DUN)
- Estonia: Estonian Network for Educational Development (ENED)
- Ethiopia: Education Quality Improvement Programme (EQUIP)
- Finland: Finnish Network for Developing University Teaching (PEDA-forum), 1994
- Germany: Deutsche Gesellschaft für Hochschuldidaktik (DGHD)
- India: Network for Staff and Educational Development (NetSED)
- Ireland: All Ireland Society for Higher Education (AISHE), 2000
- Israel: Israeli Network of Centers for the Advancement of Teaching in Higher Education (NCATHE)
- Japan: Japan Association for Educational Development in Higher Education (JAED)
- Netherlands: Contact Education Scientific Research (CRWO), 1963
- Norway: Norwegian Network for Higher Education (PEDNETT)
- Slovenia: Slovenian Association of Teaching in Higher Education (SATHE)
- South Africa: Higher Education Learning and Teaching Association of Southern Africa (HELTSA), started in 1980s, declined in 1990s, reborn 2005
- Spain: Red Estatal de Docencia Universitaria (RED-U)
- Sweden: Swedish Network for Educational Development (SwEd-Net), 1997
- Switzerland: Swiss Faculty Development Network (SFDN), 2000

- Thailand: Professional and Organizational Development Network of Thailand Higher Education (THAIPOD)
- United Kingdom: the Staff and Educational Development Association (SEDA), 1993
- United States of America: Professional and Organizational Development Network in Higher Education (POD Network), 1974

Currently, ICED members are seeking out and facilitating the creation of faculty development networks in numerous other countries.

Who Was Involved in the Beginning?

The people who stepped into this new profession were often seen as excellent teachers in their own right and people with a passion for improving teaching and learning at their institutions. In some cases, these people were associate deans or chairs of departments, who by their position and personal will were able to influence the growth and reinforce the importance of their faculty development centers. As a result, faculty developers come from a variety of disciplines (science, social science, psychology, educational psychology, history, engineering) and network with one another to learn methods for facilitating faculty teaching in a number of disciplines. These first developers were eager to share their ideas and materials with anyone who needed or wanted them. This openness and collegiality are hallmarks of the profession such that it is not unusual for first-time conference attendees to feel welcomed and amazed at this sharing, helpful atmosphere. (Current faculty developers are sometimes worried that the wonderful variety of people will be stifled if a program or training course is required for new developers.) The passion of these pioneers of teaching and learning development for what they were doing has endured throughout the years.

Teaching and Learning Center Staffing and Reporting Lines

Staffing in teaching and learning centers is typically smaller in number than one would like. Moses (1987, p. 455) indicated that in Australian universities there is a

> direct connection between the center's position in the university and its staffing: those centers which are schools or departments, and thus can also supervise postgraduate students, are more adequately staffed, and are staffed with academics. The ratio between academics in units and academics in teaching-research positions in departments varied widely; it is, for example, at the old and traditional university, University of Queensland, 1:284, at Griffith University, a small, new and non-traditional university in the same city, 1:24.

NEW DIRECTIONS FOR TEACHING AND LEARNING • DOI: 10.1002/tl

Gosling (2001) reports that the overall average size of development units in the United Kingdom is 10.3 full-time equivalents. However, institutions there are divided into two subsets: pre-1992 (older, established institutions) and post-1992 (newer, more flexible institutions). The pre-1992 universities typically had fewer full-time equivalents (approximately 8.7) in their units than did the post-1992 universities (approximately 13.1). As such, encouraging older, established institutions to see the importance of faculty development is more difficult than assisting the newer, more flexible institutions to embrace it.

A large number of centers in small to medium institutions in the United States often have one part-time director/coordinator and perhaps a part-time clerical staff person with several student assistants. Even in some large institutions, the center staff may consist of only three or four professionals, one clerical person, and three or four graduate student assistants. Other large institutions have many more staff members and administrative support, as with the Center for Research in Learning and Teaching at the University of Michigan, which has twenty-four staff members of which twelve have a doctorate.

Sell and Chism (1991) looked at the advantages and disadvantages of various staffing alternatives and found that full-time professionals were preferred for those institutions able to afford the option. The advantages brought to faculty development programs by full-time specialists include more stability and continuity, full-time commitment to the function of the center, professional training and experience as a faculty developer, and greater commitment to professional growth and activity in the faculty development field.

One trend in North America is to combine centers for teaching and learning with centers for instructional technology, educational assessment centers, audiovisual centers, and sometimes libraries. This has been done, for example, at the University of Texas at Austin such that the new Division of Instructional Innovation and Assessment has approximately ninety staff members (combined Center for Teaching Effectiveness, Center for Instructional Technology, and the Measurement and Evaluation Center). These staff members collaborate on major colloquia or seminars, work together on research studies to inform practice, work with faculty on Scholarship of Teaching and Learning (SoTL) projects and innovative technology applications, offer credit-by-exam and placement testing services for students as well as test scanning services for faculty, coordinate the student evaluation of teaching process, provide individual consultation services and workshops for faculty and graduate students, and assist the institution and departments with compliance for national or regional accrediting organizations. As you can see, there is a great deal of variety resulting from this merger (for diagrams of some of the structural models of centers, see Lewis, 1998, pp. 726–729).

Conclusion

In 1991, Derek Bok, president emeritus of Harvard University, summed up why faculty development programs need to be a part of institutions of higher education:

> The fact is that many faculty members need help, and efforts to give such help must play an important part in any comprehensive program to improve the quality of instruction. Furthermore, even if professors teach well at the moment they are tenured, there is no guarantee that they will continue to do so during their decades of service thereafter. Something more must be done to encourage and reward good instruction throughout the whole career cycle [p. 239].

Faculty development personnel and programs can facilitate continuous improvement in teaching and learning in higher education. As the role of the faculty developer continues to evolve, as suggested in the chapter by Dawson, Mighty, and Britnell in this volume, developers can affect change beyond the individual to a campuswide level. Though much research still needs to be done in this field, it is a growing, developing, and exciting area with potential for transforming teaching and learning in higher education.

References

Bartlett, T. "The Unkindest Cut." *Chronicle of Higher Education*, Mar. 22, 2002. Retrieved from http://chronicle.com/article/The-Unkindest-Cut/21885/.

Bok, D. "The Improvement of Teaching." *Teachers College Record*, 1991, 93(2), 236–251.

Brew, A., and Boud, D. "Preparing for New Academic Roles: A Holistic Approach to Development." *International Journal for Academic Development*, 1996, 1(2), 17–25.

Centra, J. A. *Faculty Development Practices in United States Colleges and Universities.* (Project Report 76–30). Princeton, N.J.: Educational Testing Service, 1976.

Crawley, A. L. "Faculty Development Programs at Research Universities: Implications for Senior Faculty Renewal." *To Improve the Academy: Resources for Faculty, Instructional, and Organizational Development*, 1995, 14, 65–90.

Glenn, D. "Wary of Budget Knife, Teaching Centers Seek to Sharpen Their Role." *Chronicle of Higher Education*, Aug. 18, 2009. Retrieved [January 5, 2010] from http://chronicle.com/article/Wary-of-Budget-Knife-Teach/48049/%20%20home%3Enews%3Efaculty.

Gosling, D. "Educational Development Units in the United Kingdom—What Are They Doing Five Years On?" *International Journal for Academic Development*, 2001, 6(1), 74–88.

Gosling, D. "Educational Development in 2006, Report of the Heads of Educational Development Group, Survey of Educational Development Units in the UK 2006." Unpublished Report. United Kingdom: Heads of Education Development Group and David Gosling (copyright holders), November 2006.

Gosling, D. "Educational Development in the UK: A Complex and Contradictory Reality." *International Journal for Academic Development*, 2009, 14(1), 5–18.

Gosling, D., and Hannan, A. "Responses to a Policy Initiative: The Case of Centers for Excellence in Teaching and Learning." *Studies in Higher Education*, 2007, *32*(5), 633–646.

Graff, J. G., & Simpson, R. D. "Faculty Development In the United States." *Innovative Higher Education*, 1994, *18*(3), 167–176.

Hicks, O. "Integration of Central and Departmental Development: Reflections from Australian Universities." *International Journal for Academic Development*, 1999, *4*(1), 43–51.

International Consortium for Educational Development—Member Organisations. Retrieved [January 5, 2010] from http://www.osds.uwa.edu.au/iced.

Justice, D. O. "The Future of Faculty Development." *POD Quarterly*, Spring 1979, *1*(1), 33–42.

Lewis, K. G. "Faculty Development in the United States: A Brief History." *International Journal for Academic Development*, 1996, *1*(2), 26–33.

Lewis, K. G. "Instructional Improvement in Higher Education." In G. R. Firth and E. F. Pajak (eds.), *Handbook of Research on School Supervision*. New York: Simon and Schuster Macmillan, 1998.

Moses, I. "Educational Development Units: A Cross-Cultural Perspective" *Higher Education*, 1987, *16*, 449–479.

North, J., and Scholl, S. C. "POD: The Founding of a National Network." *POD Quarterly*, 1979, *1*(1), 10–11.

Ouellett, M. L. (2010). "Overview of Faculty Development: History and Choices." In K. J. Gillespie, D. L. Robertson, and Associates (eds.) *A Guide to Faculty Development* (2nd ed.). San Francisco: Jossey-Bass.

Roxå, T., and Mårtensson, K. "Strategic Educational Development: A National Swedish Initiative to Support Change in Higher Education." *Higher Education Research and Development*, 2008, *27*(2), 155–168.

Sell, G. R., and Chism, N. V. "Finding the Right Match: Staffing Faculty Development Centers." *To Improve the Academy: Resources for Faculty, Instructional, and Organizational Development*, 1991, *10*, 19–29.

Sorcinelli, M. D., Austin, A. E., Eddy, P. L., and Beach, A. L. *Creating the Future of Faculty Development: Learning from the Past, Understanding the Present*. Bolton, Mass.: Anker, 2006.

Sullivan, L. (1983). "Faculty development: A movement on the brink." *The College Board Review, 127*, 21, 29–31.

Wright, W. A. (ed.). *Teaching Improvement Practices: Successful Strategies for Higher Education*. Bolton, Mass.: Anker, 1995.

Wright, W. A., and O'Neil, M. C. "Teaching Improvement Practices: International Perspectives." In W. Wright and Associates (eds.), *Teaching Improvement Practices: Successful Strategies for Higher Education*. Bolton, Mass.: Anker, 1995.

KARRON G. LEWIS *is associate director of instructional consultation and research in the Division of Instructional Innovation and Assessment (DIIA) at the University of Texas at Austin. Her research interests include strategies for interpreting student evaluations and looking at student motivation for completing them, analysis of teacher-student interactions in the classroom, and analyzing how faculty use teaching evaluations to improve their teaching.*

NEW DIRECTIONS FOR TEACHING AND LEARNING • DOI: 10.1002/tl

2

Recognizing that educational development is an important strategic lever for ensuring institutional quality, this chapter examines aspects of the careers of educational developers, including the kinds of positions they hold, the influences on their educational practice, and the factors that affect their programmatic priorities.

Educational Developers: The Multiple Structures and Influences That Support Our Work

Mary Deane Sorcinelli, Ann E. Austin

Globalization of higher education is developing at a relentless pace as colleges, universities, and student enrollments burgeon throughout countries in Africa, Asia, Eastern Europe, Latin America, and the Middle East. As a result, educational developers in Australia, Canada, Europe, and the United States, all of which have well-established higher education contexts and educational development programs, are increasingly called on to share and exchange expertise and experience with colleagues in emerging contexts.

As faculty members and faculty developers with more than fifty years of collective experience in higher education in the United States and internationally, we believe that educational development is a key strategic lever for ensuring institutional quality and supporting institutional change around the globe. We also believe that professional preparation and continued development of practitioners in the field merits attention so that developers can better support faculty and institutions in their efforts to grow and change.

In this chapter, then, we look at several aspects of educational developers' career pathways in a context where educational development has been in place for a number of years. To do so, we draw on findings from an in-depth study of educational development professionals in North America (Sorcinelli, Austin, Eddy, and Beach, 2006). Specifically, we surveyed developers from the United States and Canada who were members of the

NEW DIRECTIONS FOR TEACHING AND LEARNING, no. 122, Summer 2010 © Wiley Periodicals, Inc.
Published online in Wiley InterScience (www.interscience.wiley.com) • DOI: 10.1002/tl.395

oldest and largest professional association for educational development scholars and practitioners in North America, the Professional and Organizational Development (POD) Network in Higher Education. Formed in 1974, POD's membership currently includes educational developers from some forty countries, with the largest membership in the United States and Canada. From the outset, POD's purpose has been to support improvement in higher education through faculty, instructional, and organizational development activities.

In our study, we addressed several key questions: What are the structural variations among educational development programs (typically called faculty development in the United States)? What goals, purposes, and resources guide and influence our work? What are the top challenges facing faculty members, institutions, and educational development programs? What are new directions for the field of educational development? In this chapter, we closely examine the demographics and key dimensions of the career paths of educational developers in the United States and Canada, including their range of titles, positions, and length of time on the job. We also identify the organizations and literatures that influence and shape their work, programs, and practices.

Introduction to Our Study of Educational Developers

Overall, we learned that U.S. and Canadian educational developers represent a truly eclectic group of professionals with varied types of appointments, structural contexts, goals, and influences on their work. This finding corresponds with the conclusions of other researchers who have studied international educational development (Chism, Gosling, and Sorcinelli, 2010; Gosling, 2008; Gosling, McDonald, and Stockley, 2007; Fraser, 2005). At the same time, we did find commonalities among developers across North America. We hope that sharing our findings helps to advance an international perspective on pathways into educational development. We also hope that our findings offer suggestions for how institutions and professional associations can support educational developers as they progress in their careers, regardless of where in the world they practice.

A few issues concerning our study require special note. The individuals we studied were members of the POD Network in Higher Education. The survey was sent to the full POD mailing list (999 names). We received completed surveys from 494 developers at three hundred higher education institutions in the United States and thirty-one institutions in Canada, for an overall response rate to the survey of 50 percent. Fifty-three percent of Canadian POD members responded, as did 49 percent of U.S. POD members. Thirty-nine percent of the respondents were men and 61 percent were women. We recognize that this census of educational developers does not necessarily represent the scope and proportion of all educational development professionals around the globe. At the same time, it is representative

NEW DIRECTIONS FOR TEACHING AND LEARNING • DOI: 10.1002/tl

of the membership of the field's largest professional organization in North America.

Titles and Experience in Educational Development

We wanted to know all of the titles educational developers held at their institutions, as well as which title they considered primary. We were also interested in how long educational developers had held a position of responsibility in educational development.

Multiple Positions. We learned that it is not unusual for individuals responsible for educational development at U.S. and Canadian institutions to occupy more than one professional position. For example, one-third (33 percent) of the respondents listed their primary title as "director" of educational development. Almost one-quarter (21 percent) identified their faculty role as primary, and a similar percentage (23 percent) identified themselves as senior administrators (for example, associate provost, associate vice chancellor) or midlevel administrators (academic dean, associate dean, department chair). Almost three-quarters (70 percent) of the respondents reported holding two titles. The most prevalent combinations of titles were "director" or "associate/assistant director" and "faculty member," with 60 percent of respondents indicating they were a director of a center also holding a faculty appointment. We surmise that educational developers with faculty status as well as an administrative title are more likely to carry credibility on issues of teaching and learning because of their direct involvement in the classroom.

Length of Time in Educational Development. When we examined the length of time educational developers had held a position of responsibility in the field, our study suggested that current educational development professionals were quite new to the field. In analyzing our data, we categorized "new developers" as individuals with five or fewer years of experience and "experienced developers" as those with more than ten years of experience. Overall, more than half of the respondents clustered in the new-developers category. Only about a quarter fell into the category of experienced developers.

Length of Time in Primary Role. We then looked at respondents' number of years in educational development, organized according to their primary title and responsibility. Among directors of educational development programs, a surprisingly large group (43 percent) had five or fewer years of educational development experience. Thus a large percentage of respondents who are relatively new to educational development hold the title of director. Likewise, well over half of associate and assistant directors (56 percent), program coordinators (66 percent), midlevel administrators (72 percent), and faculty members (61 percent) also had five or fewer years of experience. Of respondents with more than ten years of experience, the majority were in positions other than director of educational development.

NEW DIRECTIONS FOR TEACHING AND LEARNING • DOI: 10.1002/tl

Only about one-third of directors (33 percent) had more than ten years of experience; the same was true for senior-level administrators (31 percent) responsible for guiding educational development efforts.

The amount of experience educational developers reported was less than we predicted and this pattern held even for developers in leadership positions (for example, directors and associate directors). The high percentage of inexperienced developers may reflect the extensive recent growth of educational development centers and programs in the United States and Canada. Other international studies also support an image of educational development "on the move." Chism (2008) found that the proportion of educational developers who assumed their first development position without prior experience in educational development seemed to be much more common in North America than in other regions of the world (for example, Australia, United Kingdom).

Although a large number of developers in the United States and Canada are new to the field, it is important to note that about one-quarter of those who chose "director" (24 percent) or "senior level administrator" (23 percent) as their primary title have been involved in educational development for more than fifteen years. Recently, some directors of centers have moved into positions such as associate provost, vice chancellor, and advisor to the president. These titles suggest legitimization of educational development as central to the mission of an institution. Thus novices can draw advice from a small cadre of seasoned colleagues.

Differences by Professional Training. Technology is one of the most compelling issues in higher education overall and in educational development in particular. Developers are deeply concerned about and engaged in issues of technology and teaching, yet we noted that only a small fraction (1 percent) of our survey respondents identified their primary title as "technology coordinator." It may be that technology coordinators involved in educational development are largely affiliated with other professional associations, or they are located in information technology or other technology-oriented campus departments and thus were not captured as part of our study. At the same time, the small percentage of educational developers who identified themselves as technology coordinators raises the question of whether—and how—educational development programs are incorporating technological issues into their concerns about teaching and learning. Not surprisingly, the technology coordinators who did respond to the survey are the newest in the field of educational development; none reported more than ten years of experience.

Influences on Individual Practice of Educational Developers

Our study also examined the sources from which developers derive their ideas. We asked developers to indicate the extent to which a number of potential sources of information, research, networking, and professional development provided through literature and organizations contributed to their "ideas about educational development practice." Respondents rated the influence of a list of possible sources (which included various publications and associations) on a 1-to-4 scale (1 = not at all, 4 = greatly influences). Means using this scale will be reported later in the chapter.

Literature Influences. Overall, educational developers agreed on the most important influences on their practice. Interestingly, they reported that their practices were influenced more by literature than by professional or scholarly organizations. The literature developers were asked to consider pertained to these topics: higher education, college teaching and learning, adult and continuing education, human resources and personal development, educational development (for example, POD or STLHE, that is, Society for Teaching and Learning in Higher Education, literature), organizational development, and disciplinary teaching journals. Within this volume, Lynn Taylor's chapter offers a lens on the relationship between educational development and disciplinary knowledge.

Educational development literature has expanded greatly over the last decade with the advent of new journals, newsletters, and handbooks on teaching, learning, and faculty motivation and development. Menges, Weimer, and Associates (1999) argue that such new scholarship can inform the practice of instruction, increase the value of teaching for those who do it, and promote changes in the faculty role, largely in response to new realities and challenges. The literature shows too that critical new findings can inform and enhance day-to-day practice not only in the classroom but also in educational development centers.

Developers found that the literature on college teaching and learning (mean: 3.64); the literature in educational development, such as POD and STLHE publications (mean: 3.47); and the literature in higher education (mean: 3.36) contributed most to their ideas about educational development and influenced their practice. Not surprisingly, educational developers rely primarily on literature that can help them and the faculty members with whom they work to think more creatively and systematically about teaching and learning processes. Such literature can include guidelines for planning, providing, evaluating, and improving instruction, as well as the results of research on learners and the learning process. Developers can use literature on teaching and learning in a variety of ways (among them bringing articles with practical ideas to the attention of new faculty members, offering suggestions for professional reading to experienced colleagues seeking to engage in innovative practices, and seeding committees charged with the leadership of institutional projects with a range of ideas reported in the literature). Similarly, the literature in educational development and in higher education can provide useful resources on educational development programs, development as teachers, development as individuals, career development, and organizational development. Developers turn to professional and scholarly literature as a source to support their own ongoing professional development.

We note that Canadian developers are influenced more by the literature in adult and continuing education (mean: 3.03) than developers in the United States (mean: 2.45), perhaps due to the strong Canadian literature and research base in this domain and the quality of "adult-centered" colleges and universities in Canada (Mancuso, 2001). We also note that a key difference between educational development in the United States and Canada and in other English-speaking countries lies in the literature that has been most influential, particularly scholarly and practice-based literature from the United Kingdom and Australia (Chism, Gosling, and Sorcinelli, 2010).

Professional Association Influences. The respondents were also asked to use the same scale to rate the influence of various associations on their thinking and practice. Those associations included national higher education associations, professional educational development associations, disciplinary or interdisciplinary associations, and regional educational development consortia.

Overall, North American educational developers most used the intellectual and collegial resources of educational development associations. They indicated the value of the POD Network in Higher Education (U.S. mean: 3.41; Canadian mean: 3.14). However, Canadian faculty developers gave their highest rating to their own professional association, the STLHE (3.53). Both POD and STLHE conferences are attended by educational developers, faculty across the disciplines, administrators, students, and staff. Their conferences and publications also address issues critical to academic affairs and undergraduate reform agendas: teaching, learning, curriculum, assessment, diversity, faculty roles, and the pedagogic aspects of technology.

Influences by Career Stage and Experience. When the ratings of influences on educational development practices were examined by the primary title of the respondent, a number of interesting differences emerged. Senior administrators rated the broad literature in higher education more highly than literature in educational development. They differed in this from directors, assistant and associate directors, and midlevel administrators, who rely more heavily on the latter source. Senior administrators may rely on the broad literature in higher education because it may speak more to systemic, organizational change in higher education (a focus that their senior-level higher education positions may require), while educational development literature focuses more on contributing to and disseminating the body of knowledge on teaching, learning, academic career development, and educational development practices (the topics on which those focused daily on direct work with faculty most likely concentrate). Not only do more experienced educational developers seem to draw on a wider range of research and literature; they also rely more on resources in adult and continuing education and personal and organizational development, areas that new developers did not note as influential. Experienced developers also seem to have more awareness of and connections to a range of professional associations. These differences may suggest that professional educational development organizations could furnish additional online information to alert developers to the range of resources they might fruitfully explore.

International Differences. Canadian respondents reported being influenced by regional educational development consortia (mean: 3.13) far more than did American respondents (2.24). Factors of size, geography, language, and culture may help account for the influence of regional consortia among Canadian developers. For example, educational development professionals in Canada met informally for a number of years at universities across the provinces prior to forming a national educational development organization (STLHE), thus developing strong networks and highly regarded forums within as well as among the provinces (Knapper, 1985).

The modest influence of regional educational development consortia reported by American respondents was somewhat surprising. There are a number of well-regarded regional consortia (notably the Great Plains Regional Consortium on Instructional Development, the Historically Black Colleges and Universities Faculty Development Network, and the New England Faculty Development Consortium) that facilitate efforts for exchanging information on faculty and instructional development through Web sites, newsletters, annual conferences, and other activities.

At the same time, national and international associations such as POD and STLHE are characterized by greater capacity and resources than regional networks have. The ability of these associations to engage multiple constituencies, institutions, and stakeholders in higher education in multiple ways (envisioning and articulating national agendas for change, convening forums of opinion leaders, collaborating with organizations engaged in complementary work, and disseminating knowledge on teaching, learning, and academic careers) may contribute to their greater influence on thinking and practice.

Influences on Educational Development Program Goals

Because educational development programs can be influenced by the priorities of a number of stakeholders, and by issues within and outside of institutions, it is important to understand what factors influence their foci and activities.

Our survey presented developers with a list of eight potential factors that guide programming selections (drawn from our experience in educational development and current topics in the literature) and asked them to indicate the extent to which each factor influenced the focus and activities of their educational development program. The potential factors, listed here as worded in the survey, were faculty interests and concerns; priorities of department chairs and deans; priorities of senior-level institutional leaders; priorities of the director or person leading your program; immediate organizational issues, concerns, or problems; institutional strategic plan; your educational development program's strategic plan; and priorities indicated in the higher education or educational development literature.

Needs and Interests of Faculty. Overwhelmingly, the factor most influencing the foci and activities of respondents' educational development efforts were the needs and interests of faculty in their institutions (mean: 3.71). Because the primary responsibility of educational developers is to enhance the professional development of the faculty members at their institutions, their attention to faculty needs and interests is not surprising. In fact, many centers develop ongoing structures for continuously assessing faculty interests and program outcomes through a variety of means such as an advisory committee or faculty interviews, focus groups, and surveys. Such needs assessments and program reviews can be conducted internally or by an external consultant. The influence of faculty on developers' priorities is also reinforced by studies that indicate that educational development programs are most effective when they have strong faculty ownership and involvement (Sorcinelli, 2002), which helps ensure that the program remains responsive to faculty needs. Faculty engagement is also a channel for emergence of faculty who can take a leadership role in teaching development and renewal and student learning.

Priorities of Program and Institutional Leaders. Not surprisingly, the priorities of the educational development program director were also cited as a primary influence (mean: 3.16). The significant influence of program directors on the direction of programs argues for their ongoing engagement in professional development through reading, attending conferences and other training, and networking, an issue we return to later in this chapter. Educational developers were equally well aware of and responsive to the priorities of senior-level institutional leaders (mean: 3.00). An administration that is committed to the concept of educational development and takes specific actions to create and support a positive environment for teaching is as crucial as faculty involvement. Optimally, the administration lends budgetary support for the educational development center's staffing and programs. Additionally, senior academic officers give tremendous credibility and visibility to the program by participating in its activities (programs, award ceremonies, and the like) and by highlighting these activities as important to the institution and its values. The special role that academic administrators can take in fostering educational development, particularly through symbolic leadership and innovative structures for faculty incentives and rewards, has been well documented (Sorcinelli and Aitken, 1995).

Least Influential to Educational Development Goals. It is important to note that, overall, educational developers were more influenced by the interests and concerns of faculty members and the priorities of senior-level administrators than by the priorities of department chairs and deans, whose influence was only "slight" to "moderate" (mean: 2.76). There may be several reasons for this. Administrators such as chairs often rotate, so that developers must routinely make time to build relationships with new appointees. It may also be difficult for developers to gain access to midlevel administrators, who often feel overwhelmed by paperwork and administrative tasks and may not interact regularly with developers. Additionally, developers may not have extensive skills in the areas of planned change, organizational development, or leadership training, topics that are of potential interest to department chairs or other administrators. Finally, as mentioned earlier, educational developers are constrained by limits of time and resources. Nevertheless, departments and colleges within universities often have legitimate priorities that would be well served by the support of educational development expertise.

Overall, the least powerful influences on educational developers' program goals and activities were issues highlighted in the literature in higher education and educational development (mean: 2.64). We suspect that, in their day-to-day work, developers spend most of their time responding to and being influenced by faculty members and provosts rather than sorting through the mountains of information available on higher education and educational development. At the same time, literature does strongly influence individual practice, as already discussed. This finding may again suggest that educational developers, much like faculty, already have more priorities and obligations than can reasonably be met. It also suggests that, as educational developers progress in their careers, they would welcome more avenues and opportunities for scholarly reflection on practice.

Conclusion

Our study of U.S. and Canadian educational developers and their careers suggests that individuals responsible for educational development in these two countries hold multiple titles and have multiple responsibilities to go along with them. The majority of respondents identify themselves as administrators, but many hold a faculty appointment as well. Perhaps most striking, as a group they tend to be relatively new to the field, with only one-quarter reporting that they have been in educational development for a decade or more. As we face a field with relatively few senior developers and some number of them nearing retirement, we may need to create more mechanisms for peer and near-peer mentoring and support along the pathway.

This portrait of educational developers also illuminates the range of sources that influence the individual practices of educational development professionals and the goals of their programs. Across all institutions in the United States and Canada, educational developers are most influenced by the interests and concerns of faculty members, the literature on college teaching and learning, and their professional organizations. Experienced educational developers tend to be more influenced by numerous literatures and organizations than are new developers, and Canadian developers are more influenced by regional educational development consortia than those in the United States.

These findings suggest that developing the careers of educational developers themselves offers both challenges and opportunities. There is no specified route to become an educational developer; the work of educational developers is expanding and is recognized at many universities and colleges as important to the success of institutional missions and goals. Educational developers who make this work their career will need to find ways to maintain their own vitality and engage in continuous learning. They will need to find ways to stay current with rapidly expanding bodies of literature pertaining to faculty careers, adult learning, faculty work, organizational change, and teaching and learning, and to use such research to inform their practice. Educational developers will also have the responsibility to continue to expand the body of scholarly knowledge in the field.

Fortunately, the profession is increasingly aware of the need to make available skills training and professional orientation for new developers as well as venues for continuous renewal of experienced developers. For example, the large professional associations in the English-speaking countries of Australia, Canada, the United Kingdom, and the United States offer workshops prior to their annual conferences, occasional institutes, ongoing networks, and online and print resources for both new and experienced developers. New professional associations are emerging in such countries as Thailand and China. As well, international educational development has generated a wealth of resources for exchange of scholarship and practices. In particular, the International Consortium for Educational Development brings together members of professional associations for faculty developers around the world, sponsoring an international conference for developers in a new host country every other year.

Finally, as we mentioned at the start of this chapter, our research has focused on faculty development in North America. However, we have had opportunities to consult and work internationally on four continents: Asia, Africa, North America, and Europe. Our travels have given us insight into the work and careers of educational developers in a number of other countries. We conclude, along with Fraser (2005), that pivotal to understanding international education development is recognition of the "multi-layered context in which we work, the complex structures that both support and constrain our work, and the variety of processes and strategies that we develop to engage teachers, the university, and the higher education sector in educational development" (p. 1). Further exploration of the pathways, experiences, influences, and approaches of educational developers, both in countries with well-established educational development programs and in those newer to establishing faculty and educational development programs, will be important in the years to come.

References

Chism, N. V. N. "A Professional Priority: Preparing Educational Developers." Paper presented at the annual meeting of the American Educational Research Association, New York, 2008.

Chism, N. V. N., Gosling, D., and Sorcinelli, M. D. "International Faculty Development: Pursuing Our Work with Colleagues Around the World." In K. H. Gillespie and D. Robinson, (eds.), *A Guide to Faculty Development*. San Francisco: Jossey-Bass, 2010.

Fraser, K., (ed.). *Education Development and Leadership in Higher Education: Developing an Effective Institutional Strategy*. London: RoutledgeFalmer, 2005.

Gosling, D. *Educational Development in the United Kingdom*. London: Heads of Educational Development Group, 2008.

Gosling, D., McDonald, J., and Stockley, D. "We Did It Our Way! Narratives of Pathways to the Profession of Educational Development." *Educational Developments*, Nov. 2007, 8(4), 7–12.

Knapper, C. "From the Editor: Our First Newsletter." *Teaching and Learning in Higher Education: Newsletter of the Society for Teaching and Learning in Higher Education*, 1985, *1*, 1–6. Retrieved [January 22, 2010] from http://www.stlhe.ca/en/publications/newletters/STLHE% 20Newsletter%2001%201985%20Summer.pdf.

Mancuso, S. (2001). Adult-centered practices: Benchmarking study in higher education. *Innovative Higher Education*, 25(3), 165–182.

Menges, R. J., Weimer, M., and Associates. *Teaching on Solid Ground: Using Scholarship to Improve Practice*. San Francisco: Jossey-Bass, 1999.

Sorcinelli, M. D. "Ten Principles of Good Practice in Creating and Sustaining Teaching and Learning Centers." In K. H. Gillespie, L. R. Hilson, and E. C. Wadsworth (eds.), *A Guide to Faculty Development: Practical Advice, Examples, and Resources*. Bolton, Mass.: Anker, 2002.

Sorcinelli, M. D., and Aitken, N. D. "Improving Teaching: Academic Leaders and Faculty Developers as Partners." In W. A. Wright and Associates (eds.), *Teaching Improvement Practices: Successful Strategies for Higher Education*. Bolton, Mass.: Anker, 1995.

Sorcinelli, M. D., Austin, A. E., Eddy, P. L., and Beach, A. L. *Creating the Future of Faculty Development: Learning from the Past, Understanding the Present*. San Francisco: Jossey-Bass, 2006.

MARY DEANE SORCINELLI is a professor of educational policy, research, and administration and associate provost for faculty development at the University of Massachusetts Amherst. A past president of the Professional and Organizational Development (POD) Network in Higher Education, she focuses her research interests on the academic profession, faculty development in the United States and internationally, teaching improvement and evaluation, and mentoring in higher education.

NEW DIRECTIONS FOR TEACHING AND LEARNING • DOI: 10.1002/tl

ANN E. AUSTIN is a professor of higher, adult, and lifelong education and director of the Global Institute for Higher Education at Michigan State University. She is a past president of the Association for the Study of Higher Education (ASHE) and focuses her research interests on faculty careers, work in academe, organizational change, reform in doctoral education, higher education issues in developing countries, and improvement of teaching and learning in higher education.

NEW DIRECTIONS FOR TEACHING AND LEARNING • DOI: 10.1002/tl

3

The pathways of eighteen educational developers are mapped based on a Canadian university study.

Charting Pathways into the Field of Educational Development

Jeanette McDonald

Educational (academic/faculty) development is a scholarly field of study and practice that evolved from an informal set of instructional improvement activities aimed at individuals, to a broad range of services, programs, and initiatives offered at the individual, departmental, and institutional levels within post-secondary education. During its fifty-year history, the field has matured (Wright and Miller, 2000) and the professional role of educational developers has moved from the periphery to the mainstream of colleges and universities (Kahn and Baume, 2003; Baume and Kahn, 2004). At the heart of these activities is a shared value of enhancing teaching and learning, and ultimately the educational experiences of students (Wright, 2002).

Over time, the growth of the field has been documented both in the literature and at professional conferences and organizational meetings internationally (for example, the Educational Developers Caucus–Canada; the Higher Education Research and Development Society of Australasia). Indeed, educational development has undergone "a systematic exercise of mapping, describing, categorizing, and classifying the field . . . in different national contexts" (Lee and McWilliam, 2008, p. 68; for other examples, see Elvidge and others, 2003; Gosling, 2009; Lewis, 1996; McDonald and Stockley, 2008; Moses, 1987; Rowland, 2003; Sorcinelli, Austin, Eddy, and Beach, 2006; Taylor, 2005). One area that has started to receive greater attention in the last decade is the study of educational developers themselves, specifically, the manner by which they learn about, enter into, and

NEW DIRECTIONS FOR TEACHING AND LEARNING, no. 122, Summer 2010 © Wiley Periodicals, Inc.
Published online in Wiley InterScience (www.interscience.wiley.com) • DOI: 10.1002/tl.396

progress within the field (for example, Fraser, 1999; Gosling, McDonald, and Stockley, 2007; Sorcinelli, Austin, Eddy, and Beach, 2006; Stefani, 1999; Wilcox, 1997).

We know that educational developers today make up a richly diverse, eclectic community of practitioners (Weimer, 1990). They have diverse educational backgrounds and disciplinary allegiances (Chism, 2008), appointment types, positional responsibilities, orientations to practice (Land, 2001, 2004), institutional values and local contexts, career motivations, and of course pathways to the profession (see Fraser, 1999; Stefani, 1999; McDonald and Stockley, 2008). Their diversity can be attributed in part to the absence of a formalized career path to profile and shape entry to and advancement within the field—what Lynn McAlpine (2006) calls "academic structures" (for example, education credentials and an accrediting body). If we are to continue to grow and attract new faces and voices to the field in an intentional way, we need to better understand the journeys developers undertake to become and identify as developers, and the shaping factors (chance events, individual values, situational conditions) within their individual contexts that influence their individual pathways.

This chapter offers a snapshot of developer pathways from a Canadian university perspective drawing on one-on-one interviews with educational developers who, at the time of their interview, were (1) formally connected to a center and (2) actively engaged in development activities at various levels, with a range of audiences, in a variety of capacities (consultant, facilitator, designer), and for different purposes (policy development, curriculum design). This definition is purposefully broad, reflecting the variation in developer positions, staffing arrangements, program mandates, and institutional settings.

Participant Profile

The pathways discussed here reflect the context of eighteen educational developers (all white) engaged in development activities at sixteen Canadian university teaching and learning units: two discipline-specific and sixteen campuswide units. Twelve of the eighteen participants were female and all but five were Canadian-born. Geographically, they were situated across the country, reflecting the regional population of Canadian universities. All had advanced degrees in diverse disciplines (sciences, arts and humanities, social sciences), with eleven of the eighteen having completed a doctorate. Participants ranged in age from their early thirties to their late fifties, with the majority (fourteen of eighteen) dispersed almost equally among three age groups: thirty-six to forty, forty-one to forty-five, and fifty-one to fifty-five years of age. Experience in the field varied, with five having less than six years of experience (new developers), eight having six to ten years of experience, and five with more than ten years' experience

NEW DIRECTIONS FOR TEACHING AND LEARNING • DOI: 10.1002/tl

(seasoned developers). Regarding mobility, almost one-third (28 percent) had worked in at least two centers, and all but three participants had full-time appointments, the majority (89 percent) of which were at the professional staff versus faculty level.

Trajectories to Educational Development

The diversity of these developers is reflected in their trajectories into the field. In this case, six (33 percent) initially entered educational development from outside higher education, all having some mixture of teaching, administration, and professional, organizational, or curriculum development experience; the remaining twelve (67 percent) transitioned from within their institution. Of the latter group, three came from the faculty ranks, six entered directly from graduate school (whether completed or not) or a postdoctoral fellowship, and three made lateral moves from other professional, administrative, and instructional and/or advising roles. Asked about their vocation, many identified an early interest in teaching, training for a helping profession, an academic track, or some other field of professional study or practice. Only a handful did not articulate a specific calling. Their vocation, combined with a personal ethos of "helping others" or "putting students first," seeded latent receptiveness to an educational development trajectory even though their awareness of the field at the time was limited or nonexistent.

Introduction to the Field

For the graduate students, postdoctoral fellows, and at least one of the three faculty members, subjects learned about their institution's teaching and learning center, and hence gained an inkling of educational development as a field of practice and more distantly a career path through a student peer or professional colleague, an external communication (that is, a flyer in their department mailbox), or their own efforts to access instructional supports and development opportunities in their role as a teaching assistant, student, or instructor. Their motivations to connect with such a unit reflected an "interest" in teaching and personal development, combined for some with a "fear" of teaching itself or not wanting to be a "bad" teacher. Whatever the case, the underlying facilitative event connecting them to a teaching unit in the first place (and, for many, engaging in development activities) was the opportunity to teach, either because of the availability and funding of their teaching assistantship or being asked to teach or direct a course (for reasons of sabbatical or research commitments).

The other two faculty members in this sample learned about their institution's center by happenstance seeded by their engagement in scholarly teaching, and for one, discipline-based development activities with graduate students in his own department. In the former case (we'll call

NEW DIRECTIONS FOR TEACHING AND LEARNING • DOI: 10.1002/tl

him Tony), overhearing a conversation on the subject of teaching between a faculty member and the previous center director of the institution (unknown to Tony at the time) prompted him to engage in conversation asking questions about his latest "evaluation thing." Following up on resources shared by the former director, he contacted his teaching and learning unit to learn more. The second faculty member (we'll call him Sean) came to the attention of his center through a colleague who had previous center connections and who worked with Sean directly. In this case, the center came to Sean, asking him to offer a campuswide workshop to teaching assistants. Chance encounters combined with other situational happenings and personal motivations set Tony on a path to find "individuals that have an interest in teaching . . . [and] a place to go and learn about, but also just talk about teaching," and set Sean on a path to "doing . . . workshops within the TA [teaching assistants] Conference, to overseeing how the conference ran, interfering and rearranging it . . . to build[ing] up . . . different programs."

For the six developers who initially came from outside the field and higher education itself, educational development represented a second or even third career move. Their motivations to leave or augment their existing positions and areas of professional practice reflected a host of reasons: a desire to move on to the next phase of their career (challenge of something new), a need to get out of their current position (often for reasons of dissatisfaction), and the necessity of another job (that is, full-time work, end of contract). In all but one case, working in a teaching and learning center was *not* their primary goal. Only four were specifically looking for a job; the remaining two found theirs by chance. For Karen, a colleague pointed out and explained the position to her. Paul came across his first developer job posting in his regular perusal of *University Affairs,* a publication he relied on to remain current with topical issues and trends in higher education. Both saw immediate connections to the job description by way of their knowledge and skill sets, with Paul recognizing something in himself ("this is me, this is totally me").

The Journey: Critical Incidents, Facilitative Events, Influential People

The path to educational development for some was more direct, with fewer dips and curves along the way. Others had more winding routes with diversions and barriers to overcome. In most cases, serendipity and chance played a role in their pathway. Betsworth and Hansen (1996, p. 93) define serendipity as "events that were not planned or predictable, but that had a significant influence on an individual's career," while Cabral and Salomone (1990, p. 6) define chance as "the particular people who influence an individual, as well as the timing and context within which life events occur." As the latter definition begins to suggest and as Williams and his colleagues

NEW DIRECTIONS FOR TEACHING AND LEARNING • DOI: 10.1002/tl

(1998) further support, "the interaction between such events and the person's 'readiness' to incorporate chance events into his or her career decisions" (p. 379) cannot be overlooked.

For those who had a more direct route (particularly those in graduate school or pursuing a postdoctorate), timing, fit, and the conditions under which their various chance encounters took place were primary. For some, family was an enabling or facilitative factor. Miranda, for example, moved to an institution to do her postdoctorate to be closer to home. Once there, she initiated contact with the campus teaching center, volunteering to do workshops and thereby positioning herself for an educational development job. Her graduate experience had already prompted an early and positive interest in development work, as well as a preference for the applied nature of the scholarship of teaching and learning—an aspect she found lacking in her own discipline scholarship. Norah likewise connected to development work soon after completing her doctorate. With her husband finding a faculty job first, she looked to the same institution to apply her discipline and found it in educational development, a context she was formerly connected to through a disciplinary colleague and her own participation as a graduate student and sessional instructor. Still others made the move to educational development during or just after their doctorate for such reasons as loss of interest in their discipline research, work-life balance issues, the relational aspect of development work, the inviting and welcoming community within the center and beyond (if they had experienced contact at the regional or national level), and the scope of practice and balance of responsibilities of their particular developer position. Other facilitative conditions paving the way to educational development included creation of new developer positions through investment of funds and support on the part of central administration, departure of a developer (returning to his or her discipline) making way for others to join the team, invitation by a colleague to apply for development work given previous center connections, and so on. Although their paths were more direct, they also encountered barriers and diversions along the way. For a period, Miranda led a double life as graduate student and educational developer. The latter she did "undercover" in light of her supervisor's disapproval and lack of validation for teaching development. Others likewise pointed to discouragement or the scheduling of conflicting events by their department as restrictive to their engagement in teaching development activities.

Those whose path was less direct, as noted above, experienced a few more dips and turns and took longer to commit to and find educational development, grappling for example with their allegiance within the discipline and a faculty appointment. Tara experienced this predicament after not attaining a tenured-track faculty position. As she reflected, "I didn't get the job, but at the same time I had this huge sense of relief . . . and remembered thinking at the time, 'what was that all about?'" Later in the interview she conceded that her development role just felt "more

NEW DIRECTIONS FOR TEACHING AND LEARNING • DOI: 10.1002/tl

comfortable," which she attributes in part to her director (an enabler) who "treats her as an academic" and allows her to bring together her "discipline interests" with higher education research, teaching, and service. Fida likewise struggled to make a full commitment to educational development once she entered academia and first experienced development work. Several moves across the country due to her spouse's career path and a dual interest and focus in teaching and educational development kept her from focusing on one job and area of professional focus. The latter came when she realized she was feeling burnt out in her current position, which prompted her to take proactive steps to move her career in educational development to the next level. Within an environment of greater mobility, she applied for more senior level educational development positions, noting "what a feeling of validation [she gained] from . . . those experiences."

Self-Identify as a Developer or with Educational Development

Entry into the field did not a developer make. The majority, regardless of their starting point or knowledge and skill sets, noted a period of between two and four years before settling into their role. This period of orientation and socialization can be likened to a form of apprenticeship (see Lave and Wenger, 1991) during which they learn the "living curriculum" (Wenger, 2006) of their newly ascribed community of practice (see Wenger, 1998). Norah, like others, spoke to this period of enculturation to the field:

> I think over the last three years . . . I had to learn a lot about educational development because I wasn't specifically trained for this, so a lot of what I brought in really helped me, but I had to learn a lot as well. And, so now, I feel pretty comfortable in the role, and I feel like I'm familiar with what we do and why we do it, and I feel like I know people in the field, so I became a part of the community as well.

Fortunately, varied avenues are increasingly available to aid in preparing developers for their role. For example, the Professional and Organizational Development (POD) Network in the United States offers an Institute for New Faculty Developers; the Staff and Educational Development Association in the United Kingdom offers a fellowship program to accredit those involved in educational development activities in the UK and internationally (http://www.seda.ac.uk/professional-development.html?p=3_2); and postgraduate programs in learning and cognition, for example, increasingly offer formalized modes of training (University of Texas at Austin: http://www.edb.utexas.edu/education/departments/edp/admissions/programs/doctoral/area1/).

In addition to an initial period of socialization or apprenticeship in the field, as noted earlier, a sense of validation by others (peers, director,

NEW DIRECTIONS FOR TEACHING AND LEARNING • DOI: 10.1002/tl

faculty, development community) proved to be a solidifying factor. Celine shared that

> the part where I felt it was legitimate and I felt like . . . I knew what I was doing [was when] . . . someone . . . turned to us . . . [and] asked for my opinion or my assistance in developing workshops outside of my normal routine . . . then you sort of become more aware that others are aware of what you're doing.

Breaking away from an old identity or finding a way to blend multiple identities into their concept of educational developer was critical for some also. Miranda spoke to this.

> It wasn't until I broke away from graduate school and was doing . . . work on my own that I identified as somebody with a really keen interest in educational development . . . that I started saying, "I'm an educational developer and that's what I do."

Others saw educational development as being a good fit with their interests or values. Fida, who came from outside the university context, noted: "it was reinforcing, it was validating, it was exhilarating. I very quickly found . . . it was a superb fit for my interests and my personality type, for the kinds of work that I find fulfilling." Similarly, Edward commented, "I'm always trying to do my best . . . to help other people that's sort of the bottom line. . . . It's more a philosophy of life."

Another major attraction to enter into, remain in, and identify with the field was the development community itself. For most, it imparted a sense of belonging and was a forum for engagement with others about their practice at multiple levels. Again, Wenger's notion of community of practice (1998, 2006) fits well here. Lila, for example, commented that "the preconference [workshop], that's when I really started to realize [that] . . . this is not just a contract or a teaching job, this is a career with a series of models and other people doing it." Karen reinforced the place of community, noting the importance of having "a group of people that speak the same language . . . a group that you belong to, [that] it's not something you made up." Further still, Victor reiterated,

> meeting the network of other developers, relying on them to learn the job that seemed like a temporary job, made it clear that this could be a career, and finding out that so many people had various pathways into it, finding out there were people from almost every discipline under the sun, and people who were like me [made it real to me].

Others additionally identified a point where they made a conscious decision to engage with educational development full-time and permanently. Dan acknowledged that point was "probably when I went from part-time to full-time. It was a conscious decision to do that . . . [which] meant not finishing my thesis." Miranda made a similar leap of faith when she "eventually admit[ted] to [her]self that this was the half of my double-life that I wanted to come out of the closet."

Conclusion

This snapshot only begins to scratch the surface of the varied and some-times complex journeys educational developers undertake to enter into and chart their pathway within the field of educational development. It is a necessary step, however, toward a better understanding of what attracts and sustains developers in the profession. With this information, we can more intentionally chart and promote avenues for professionals and aca-demics to enter the field, at a time when educational development practi-tioners and centers are being called on to meet individual needs and institutional, sector, national, and international mandates and agendas.

References

Baume, D., and Kahn, P. (eds.). *Enhancing Staff and Educational Development*. London: Routledge Falmer, 2004.

Betsworth, D., and Hansen, J. "The Categorization of Serendipitous Career Develop-ment Events." *Journal of Career Assessment,* 1996, *4*(1), 91–98.

Cabral, A., and Salomone, P. "Chance and Careers: Normative Versus Contextual Development." *Career Development Quarterly,* 1990, *39,* 5–7.

Chism, N. "A Professional Priority: Preparing Educational Developers." Paper presented at the annual meeting of the American Educational Research Association (AERA), New York, Mar. 25, 2008.

Elvidge, L., Fraser, K., Land, R., Mason, C., and Matthew, B. (eds.). *Exploring Academic Development in Higher Education: Issues of Engagement.* Cambridge, UK: Jill Rogers Associates, 2003.

Fraser, K. "Australasian Academic Developers: Entry into the Profession and Our Own Professional Development." *International Journal for Academic Development,* 1999, *4*(2), 89–101.

Gosling, D. "Educational Development in the UK: A Complex and Contradictory Real-ity." *International Journal for Academic Development,* 2009, *14*(1), 5–18.

Gosling, D., McDonald, J., and Stockley, D. "We Did It Our Way! Narratives of Path-ways to the Profession of Educational Development." *Educational Developments,* 2007, *8*(4), 1–6.

Kahn, P., and Baume, D. (eds.). *A Guide to Staff and Educational Development.* London: Kogan Page, 2003.

Land, R. "Agency, Context and Change in Academic Development." *International Jour-nal for Academic Development,* 2001, *6*(1), 4–20.

Land, R. *Educational Development: Discourse, Identity and Practice.* Buckingham, UK: Society for Research into Higher Education and Open University Press, 2004.

Lave, J., and Wenger, E. *Situated Learning: Legitimate Peripheral Participation.* Cam-bridge, UK: Cambridge University Press, 1991.

Lee, A., and McWilliam, E. "What Game Are We In? Living with Academic Develop-ment." *International Journal for Academic Development,* 2008, *13*(1), 67–77.

Lewis, K. G. "Faculty Development in the United States: A Brief History." *International Journal for Academic Development,* 1996, *1*(2), 26–33.

McAlpine, L. "Coming of Age in a Time of Super-Complexity (with Apologies to Both Mead and Barnett)." *International Journal for Academic Development,* 2006, *11*(2), 123–127.

McDonald, J., and Stockley, D. "Pathways to the Profession of Educational Development: An International Perspective." *International Journal for Academic Development,* 2008, *13*(3), 213–218.

Moses, I. "Educational Development Units: A Cross-Cultural Perspective." *Higher Education,* 1987, *16,* 449–479.

Rowland, S. "Academic Development: A Practical or Theoretical Business." In H. Eggins and R. Macdonald (eds.), *The Scholarship of Academic Development.* Buckingham, UK: Society for Research into Higher Education and Open University Press, 2003.

Sorcinelli, M. D., Austin, A. E., Eddy, P. L., and Beach, A. L. *Creating the Future of Faculty Development: Learning from the Past, Understanding the Present.* Bolton, Mass.: Anker, 2006.

Stefani, L. "On Becoming an Academic Developer: A Personal Journey." *International Journal for Academic Development,* 1999, *4*(2), 102–110.

Taylor, K. L. "Academic Development as Institutional Leadership: An Interplay of Person, Role, Strategy, and Institution." *International Journal for Academic Development,* 2005, *10*(1), 31–46.

Weimer, M. *Improving College Teaching: Strategies for Developing Instructional Effectiveness.* San Francisco: Jossey-Bass, 1990.

Wenger, E. *Communities of Practice: Learning, Meaning, and Identity.* Cambridge, UK: Cambridge University Press, 1998.

Wenger, E. "Communities of Practice: A Brief Introduction." 2006. Retrieved [February 5, 2010] from http://www.ewenger.com/theory/.

Wilcox, S. "Becoming a Faculty Developer." *New Directions for Adult and Continuing Education,* 1997, *74,* 23–31.

Williams, E., Soeprapto, E., Like, K., Touradji, P., Hess, S., and Hill, C. "Perceptions of Serendipity: Career Paths of Prominent Academic Women in Counselling Psychology." *Journal of Counselling Psychology,* 1998, *45*(4), 379–389.

Wright, D. L. "Program Types and Prototypes." In K. H. Gillespie, W. R. Hilsen, and E. C. Wadsworth (eds.), *A Guide to Faculty Development: Practical Advice, Examples and Resources.* San Francisco: Jossey-Bass, 2002.

Wright, W., and Miller, J. "The Educational Developer's Portfolio." *International Journal for Academic Development,* 2000, *5*(1), 1–5.

JEANETTE MCDONALD is manager of educational development in the Office of Teaching Support Services at Wilfrid Laurier University in Ontario, Canada.

NEW DIRECTIONS FOR TEACHING AND LEARNING • DOI: 10.1002/tl

SECTION TWO

Practice

During the almost fifty-year history of educational development, researchers have conceptualized a number of models to describe the work of the field. These models all fit within a broad conceptual framework that consists of three distinct yet overlapping approaches that are identified in this chapter.

Conceptualizing Evolving Models of Educational Development

Kym Fraser, David Gosling, Mary Deane Sorcinelli

The three authors of this chapter work in the field of educational development on three continents: Australasia, Europe, and North America. Within and between the three continents, the terminology we use to describe our often similar work varies, and so we preface our discussion with a definition of *educational development*. We use the term in this chapter to refer to the field of professional and strategic development associated with university and college learning and teaching.

Internationally, the terms used to describe this activity include "academic development," "learning and teaching development," "education development," and "faculty development." The terminology is contested and somewhat divides along United States and United Kingdom/Commonwealth lines, with "faculty development" the preferred U.S. term (Ryan and Fraser, 2010).

As Ryan and Fraser highlight, in this field we work with many types of staff across the university, not just academics or faculty, and the work ranges from policy development or implementation and research to curriculum redesign and evaluation, with many things in between. So even though we work in a diverse field with context-specific variations in terminology, practice, and clientele, we have chosen to use the term *educational development* in this chapter because we believe it reflects the scope and diversity of the field. While recognizing such variability in the field, we argue in this chapter that the models and work of educational development

NEW DIRECTIONS FOR TEACHING AND LEARNING, no. 122, Summer 2010 © Wiley Periodicals, Inc.
Published online in Wiley InterScience (www.interscience.wiley.com) • DOI: 10.1002/tl.397

can be encompassed within a consistent conceptual framework that remains valid across our three continents.

Evolving Models of Educational Development

What Is a Model of Educational Development? Researchers have used the term *model* in different ways when describing educational development. In the mid-1970s, Gaff (1975) used it to describe the type of work involved in educational development, while Clark, Corcoran, and Lewis (1986) employed it to describe the range of dimensions included in the work of educational development. Hicks (1999) applied the label model to describe the structural location of educational development in the university, while Land (2001, 2004) used the term to describe the "approach" taken to the work of educational developers.

Clearly, educational development can be described in many ways by referring to its different aspects. In this chapter we endeavor to categorize many of the models that have been used to describe educational development over the last thirty-five years. In doing so, we've chosen to situate them within a framework that consists of three broad approaches to educational development:

Educational development focused on the individual staff member
Educational development focused on the institution
Educational development focused on the sector

These three approaches appear to be most useful for categorizing often disparate models of educational development and have elements in common with the work of researchers on several continents (Ling and Council of Australian Directors of Academic Development, 2009; Sorcinelli, Austin, Eddy, and Beach, 2006). It is likely that many if not most educational development units carry out work in both of the first two approaches, individual and institutional, with many developers switching between the two approaches depending on the context in which they are working; the approaches are not exclusive of one another. The third approach to educational development is a more recent development.

Educational Development Focused on the Individual Staff Member

The term *staff* is used in this document to refer to university employees. Although "academics" or "faculty" often stand in, this term also may include support staff who assist students in learning, such as library, academic skills, career, information technology, student services, equity, and disability staff. From its inception, educational development has worked with individual staff members and even though, over time, the focus of work has expanded in many universities to include the institutional and sector approaches mentioned above, most educational developers continue to work at the individual level. In this approach the educational developer generally works with one or a small group of staff to provide information and develop skills associated with specific aspects and contexts of teaching, for example use of information technology, teaching of large groups, and implementation of assessment processes. We next describe some of the models that include this "teacher"-focused approach.

In the mid-1970s in the United States, Bergquist and Phillips (1975) suggested a model with three complementary approaches to educational development, two of which fall within the individual-staff-member approach. *Instructional development* focuses on the *process* of education and the design of courses; it includes evaluating course organization, presentation skills, and effectiveness through such means as class visits, videotaping, and student feedback. Programs include identification of course goals and teaching methods, broader curriculum development, and media design components. *Personal development* includes programs to promote individual personal growth, life planning, and interpersonal skills.

In the United Kingdom, Boud and McDonald (1981) suggested there were three models of educational development, all focused on working with individuals or groups of staff: *professional service, counseling, and collegial.* The professional service model sees educational development as providing specialized services such as computer-assisted learning, instructional design, and diversifying assessment. Some United Kingdom and Australasian educational development centers continue to see themselves as essentially an academic support service, and this model resembles the instructional development component in Bergquist and Phillips's model (1975).

Second, the counseling model seeks to "help teachers reach an understanding of how they might be able to deal with problems which they have identified" (Boud and McDonald, 1981, p. 5). This approach involves working with individual teachers to assist them in, for example, adjusting to changes in their institution, or to challenges they face in their teaching. Its aim is to support academics in their personal and professional development and enable them to grow in their role and achieve personal fulfilment. This model connects closely with the personal development component of Bergquist and Phillips's model (1975).

Third, the collegial model, which appears in literature in both the United Kingdom and the United States, is associated with a "collegial" ideal of higher education and sees educational development as focused on collaboration with academics in joint projects to improve practice, for example through action research, peer review of teaching, and design of new materials for online learning (Becher and Kogan, 1992; McNay, 1995).

More recently, Gosling (1997) and Land (2001, 2004), both UK academics, have described a model of educational development that focuses on achieving professional competency for all teaching staff. It is a reaction

NEW DIRECTIONS FOR TEACHING AND LEARNING • DOI: 10.1002/tl

to what is perceived to be a lack of professional preparation of academics, who traditionally have expertise in research rather than teaching. This approach is dominated by a concern to protect students from "bad" teaching. The growth of initial teaching professional development programs for new academics (now compulsory in some countries such as the United Kingdom) is a reflection of the desire to ensure that all those involved in teaching or supporting student learning have a minimum level of competence that can be certified through formal professional accreditation.

Land (2001, 2004) suggests that some educational developers oppose this competency model because of its implicit deficit view of academics' teaching skills and that many of these developers might instead adopt what he calls a "romantic" model that supports each individual's expertise and experience. He also identifies an *internal consultant* model, which offers the expert knowledge of the educational developer to individuals and departments to help them achieve their goals, while a *modeler-broker* alternative acts as a conduit or communicator between levels of the institution.

Almost from the outset of educational development in Australia and the United States, and becoming popular more recently in the United Kingdom, is the *educational researcher* model, in which the function of educational development is similar to that of an academic department in that developers undertake research specializing in pedagogy, institutional research, and higher education more broadly (Gosling, 1997; Land, 2001, 2004). The Scholarship of Teaching and Learning (SoTL) movement (Hutchings and Shulman, 1999) built on this approach by emphasizing that teaching and learning in higher education is a complex social activity worthy of systematic investigation.

Toombs (1975) and Gaff (1975) independently enhanced the Bergquist and Phillips model when they suggested that educational development programs also needed to be built around the career span of staff. Their work led to considerable research in this area in the United States. For example, Baldwin and Blackburn's research (1981) identified five career stages: new assistant professors in their first three years of college teaching, assistant professors with more than three years of college teaching experience, associate or midcareer professors, full professors more than five years from retirement, and full professors within five years of formal retirement. On the basis of their findings, Baldwin and Blackburn suggested that institutions of higher education should anticipate that academics at different career stages may have varying needs and be more or less responsive to several types of support. They urged that institutions maintain the flexibility necessary to encourage professional growth because academics may become "stuck" at one career phase and not move forward. They also posited that institutions needed to broaden their focus beyond assistance with teaching to include professional, organizational, and personal development of academics.

Educational Development Focused on the Institution or Organization

Individually oriented approaches to educational development have been criticized as having limited impact: "The dominant orientation of these [educational development] centers to individuals rather than to program or process improvement involving groups of faculty members limits their contribution to 'organisational' learning" (Dill, 2005, p. 139).

Dill contrasts an approach that supports individual academics with one focusing on institutional change. Trowler and Bamber (2005) further criticize educational developers for "relying on individual change" because they say this approach "commits the error of 'methodological individualism' . . . ; it exaggerates the power of agency over that of structure, seeing individual actors as the prime movers and shakers in social change" (p. 84). In this section, we contend that educational development has included organizational development and institutional change in its earliest models; however, contributing to organizational as well as individual change remains an ongoing concern for the field.

By the start of the twenty-first century, many universities on all three continents had begun to include an institutional or organizational approach to educational development. Theories of organization change and management (Rossiter, 2007) underpinned many of the models of educational development that focused on institutional change. Educational development units were increasingly tasked with facilitating implementation of strategic plans (for example, learning and teaching operational plans) and improving achievement against performance indicators such as student satisfaction and student learning outcomes (Ling, 2005). Educational development was aligned with institutional needs and priorities as defined by the senior management processes of the university. Educational development arguably became a function of strategic leadership, with units often structurally located within human resource departments, or as part of the vice principal's office, and tasked with achieving higher efficiency and effectiveness (Gosling, 2009; Ling and Council of Australian Directors of Academic Development, 2009).

In the United States, Bergquist and Phillips (1975), Toombs (1975), and Gaff (1975) had argued for such an approach in the mid-1970s, long before universities had strategic learning and teaching plans. They proposed organizational development as a third and key component of their educational development model. In their view, organizational development included policies and practices that created an effective institutional environment for teaching and learning. Activities might include administrative development for chairs, deans, and other academic leaders, and establishment of policies such as evaluation and recognition of teaching in the reward structure.

In 1986, Clark, Corcoran, and Lewis proposed an approach to educational development in the United States that focused directly on the institutional environment and the responsibilities of the institution for development of its academics. They argued that "academic," "institutional vitality," and "institutional mission" were interrelated concepts. They urged that educational development programs support scholarly and instructional development of academics and provide differentiated support for new, midcareer, and senior academics. The authors concluded that the field of educational development must learn more about adult development theory, professional socialization of academics, how their careers are structured, and how academic institutions affect academic vitality in order to create and sustain worthwhile educational development programs.

In the United Kingdom, Land's *political-strategic* and *opportunist* models (2001, 2004) both looked for ways to take advantage of the existing institutional context. The former was more strategic (with clear goals in mind) while the latter was more pragmatic. Land's *entrepreneur* model (2004) was seen to be opportunistic, taking advantage of sources of funding and seeing educational development as meeting internal and external needs by offering high-demand services (web design, publications, conferences, workshops).

The new millennium ushered in a new approach to educational development that transcended individual institutions and focused across the higher education sector and therefore across institutions.

Educational Development Focused on the Sector

Since the start of the twenty-first century, there has already been emphasis in many countries on the accountability of universities to the public for the quality of their teaching and student outcomes. In large part, this change has been a consequence of the growing number and diversity of students, and in the United Kingdom and Australia introduction of university fees. With these changes came public and government concern about the quality of the student learning experience (Smith, 2005; Sorcinelli, Austin, Eddy, and Beach, 2006). Subsequently, demands for accountability required universities to demonstrate "systematic improvement in support for learning and teaching, and at least minimal development programs for staff" (Ryan and Fraser, 2010).

Public and government concern led to constitution of national quality assurance agencies such as the United Kingdom Quality Assurance Agency and the Australian Universities Quality Agency. Both continue to evolve over time, and their focus has moved recently to quality assurance of programs, in particular through implementation of standards frameworks such as the United Kingdom National Professional Standards Framework for Teaching and Supporting Learning in Higher Education: "National funding bodies, such as the Australian Learning and Teaching Performance Fund, while controversial, reward institutions for learning performance outcomes" (Ryan and Fraser, 2010).

In many countries, public scrutiny resulted in constitution of national agencies that had a mandate to improve "the student learning experience by supporting quality teaching and practice" (Australian Learning and Teaching Council Mission, http://www.altc.edu.au/who-we-are). National teaching and learning institutes such as the United Kingdom Higher Education Academy, New Zealand's Ako Aotearoa, and the Australian Learning and Teaching Council were constituted after the turn of the century. These organizations sought to create sectorwide change by funding projects to study sector and disciplinewide teaching and learning issues, introducing national centers of excellence, developing discipline networks, and recognizing excellent teachers and programs.

Since its inception, the Australian Learning and Teaching Council has awarded more than two hundred grants for learning and teaching investigation projects, providing more than $37 million in funding. The grants have been awarded through four programs: competitive grants, leadership, priority projects, and discipline studies programs. Teaching excellence has been recognized and rewarded through five programs: citations for outstanding contributions to student learning, awards for programs that enhance learning, awards for teaching excellence, the prime minister's award for Australian University Teacher of the Year, and the Career Achievement Award. More than $8 million has been furnished over four years to these awards. Predecessors of the Australian Learning and Teaching Council existed from the early 1990s and have also invested many millions of dollars on development of teaching initiatives in higher education.

In the United Kingdom, the Teaching Quality Enhancement Fund was established by the Higher Education Funding Council for England, with the declared aims of enhancing the quality of teaching and learning and raising the status of teaching among higher education institutions. The initiative had three strands—subject, institutional, and individual—from which emerged the Learning and Teaching Subject Centers, National Teaching Fellowships, and the requirement that all institutions have learning and teaching strategies (Gosling, 2004). In 2004, £340 million was invested in establishing seventy-four Centers for Excellence in Teaching and Learning.

In North America, Canada created the 3M National Teaching Fellowships in 1986. These awards recognize teaching excellence and educational leadership in student learning. There are now more than two hundred 3M National Teaching Fellows scattered throughout Canada, representing a broad range of academic disciplines. Various bodies and task forces in the United States, such as the U.S. Department of Education and its recent Commission on the Future of Higher Education, the Association of American Colleges and Universities, the Carnegie Foundation for the

Advancement of Teaching, and the National Science Foundation, have moved forward development of the student learning experience in higher education by establishing policies related to higher education, overseeing research and collecting data on America's colleges and universities, providing grant and award opportunities, and identifying and drawing attention to major issues in higher education.

National educational development professional bodies have been constituted in Canada (Educational Developers Caucus), the United Kingdom (United Kingdom Higher Education Development Group), and Australia (the Council of Australian Directors of Academic Development). In particular the Australian national body appears unique currently in that in the last two years it has accessed unprecedented funding from national sources to make progress in research into sectorwide teaching and learning issues.

All of these developments nationally and internationally have spurred the evolution of an educational development model of sectorwide scholarship and teaching practice change. Even though this model of educational development holds a lot of promise for effective use of scarce resources to effect change, we are cognizant of the many barriers to the uptake of this work within institutions and programs.

Conclusion

Approaches to educational development have evolved over the fifty-year history of the field, with many educational development units using several approaches in their work, depending on the local context. Although a range of educational development models have been proposed and described over time, we suggest that most if not all are encompassed within a consistent conceptual framework, grounded by three approaches to educational development focused on the individual, the institution, and the sector.

In taking a reflective look at models of educational development, one finds that in the 1970s and early 1980s theorists classified the field into several overlapping dimensions: personal, counseling, and academic development; instructional, professional, and curricular development; collegial; and organizational development. The literature further evolved when researchers in the 1980s advocated matching educational development activities with various career and adult developmental stages. During that decade, researchers also called for more attention to the link between educational development and institutional development, and the need to concentrate not just on teaching but also on the broad range of academic roles and professional development needs.

In the new millennium, the evolution of sectorwide educational development holds promise for significant improvement of the student learning experience (Ryan and Fraser, 2010; Ling and Council of Australian Directors of Academic Development, 2009). As we continue to envision the future of educational development, we are optimistic that it will remain a multifaceted enterprise and a key lever for change that will assist higher education across the globe to improve individual, institutional, and sector-level teaching and learning quality.

References

Australian Learning and Teaching Council. "Who We Are." Retrieved [January 14, 2010] from http://www.altc.edu.au/who-we-are.

Baldwin, R. G., and Blackburn, R. T. "The Academic Career as a Development Process." *Journal of Higher Education,* 1981, *52*(6), 598–614.

Becher, T., and Kogan, M. *Process and Structure in Higher Education.* London: Routledge, 1992.

Bergquist, W. H., and Phillips, S. R. "Components of an Effective Faculty Development Program." *Journal of Higher Education,* 1975, *46*(2), 177–215.

Boud, D., and McDonald, R. *Educational Development Through Consultancy.* Guildford, UK: Society for Research in Higher Education (SRHE), 1981.

Clark, S. M., Corcoran, M., and Lewis, D. R. "The Case for Institutional Perspective on Faculty Development." *Journal of Higher Education,* 1986, *57*(2), 176–195.

Dill, D. D. "The Degradation of the Academic Ethic: Teaching, Research and the Renewal of Professional Self-Regulation." In R. Barnett (ed.), *Reshaping the University: New Relationships Between Research, Scholarship and Teaching.* Maidenhead, UK: Open University Press, McGraw-Hill Education, 2005.

Gaff, G. *Toward Faculty Renewal.* San Francisco: Jossey-Bass, 1975.

Gosling, D. "Educational Development and Institutional Change in Higher Education." In K. Gokulsing and C. Da Costa (eds.), *Usable Knowledges as the Goal of University Education.* Lampeter, UK: Edwin Mellen Press, 1997.

Gosling, D. "The Impact of a National Policy to Enhance Teaching Quality and Status, England, the United Kingdom." *Quality Assurance in Education,* 2004, *12*(3), 136–149.

Gosling, D. "Educational Development in the United Kingdom: A Complex and Contradictory Reality." *International Journal for Academic Development,* 2009, *14*(1), 5–18.

Hicks, O. "Integration of Central and Departmental Development: Reflections from Australian Universities." *International Journal for Academic Development,* 1999, *4*(1), 43–51.

Hutchings, P., and Shulman, L. "The Scholarship of Teaching: New Elaborations, New Developments." In D. DeZure (ed.), *Learning from Change: Landmarks in Teaching and Learning in Higher Education from Change Magazine 1969–1999.* London: Kogan Page, 1999.

Land, R. "Agency, Context and Change in Academic Development." *International Journal for Academic Development,* 2001, *6*(1), 4–20.

Land R. *Education Development: Discourse, Identity and Practice.* Maidenhead, UK: Open University Press/Society for Research in Higher Education, 2004.

Ling, P. "From a Community of Scholars to a Company." In K. Fraser (ed.), *Education Development and Leadership in Higher Education.* Abingdon, UK: RoutledgeFalmer, 2005.

Ling, P., and Council of Australian Directors of Academic Development. *Development of Academics and Higher Education Futures, Vol. 1* (report). Sydney: Australian Learning and Teaching Council, 2009.

McNay, I. "From Collegial Academy to Corporate Enterprise: The Changing Cultures of Universities." In T. Schuller (ed.), *The Changing University?* Buckingham, UK: SRHE/Open University Press, 1995.

Rossiter, D. "Whither E-learning? Conceptions of Change and Innovation in Higher Education." *Organisational Transformation and Social Change,* 2007, *4*(1), 93–107.

Ryan, Y., and Fraser, K. "Education Development in Higher Education." In McGaw, Peterson, and Baker (eds.), *The International Encyclopedia of Education, 3rd edition,* 2010, *Vol. 4,* 411–418, Elsevier, Oxford, UK.

Smith, B. "The Role of United Kingdom Organisations in Enhancing the Quality of Teaching and Learning in Higher Education." In K. Fraser (ed.), *Education Development and Leadership in Higher Education.* Abingdon, UK: RoutledgeFalmer, 2005.

Sorcinelli, M. D., Austin, A. E., Eddy, P. L., and Beach, A. L. *Creating the Future of Faculty Development.* Bolton, Mass.: Anker, 2006.

Toombs, W. "A Three-Dimensional View of Faculty Development." *Journal of Higher Education,* 1975, *46,* 701–717.

Trowler, P., and Bamber, R. "Compulsory Higher Education Teacher Training: Joined-up Policies, Institutional Architectures and Enhancement Cultures." *International Journal for Academic Development,* 2005, *10*(2), 79–93.

KYM FRASER is an associate professor at the Australian Catholic University. She edited the 2005 book Education Development in Higher Education *and wrote* Studying for Continuing Professional Development *(2009).*

DAVID GOSLING is a visiting research fellow at the University of Plymouth, United Kingdom. He is an international higher education researcher currently working on a critical history of educational development in the United Kingdom.

MARY DEANE SORCINELLI is a professor of educational policy, research, and administration and the associate provost for faculty development at the University of Massachusetts, Amherst.

5

Because the primary teaching resource of faculty members is their disciplinary expertise, it is essential that educational developers understand how their work is shaped by an appreciation of how the structure, processes, and culture of a discipline influence faculty decisions about teaching and learning.

Understanding the Disciplines Within the Context of Educational Development

K. Lynn Taylor

"Remember the time when . . . ?" Most educational developers can tell you a story of a moment when they stood in the breach between their enthusiasm for an educational concept and their ability to communicate that concept in a way that seemed meaningful to a colleague whose expertise was in a field other than teaching and learning. These are defining moments in articulating the heart of educational development practice: the moments when we find ourselves challenged to communicate our knowledge of teaching and learning in ways that are meaningful and deep in a discipline context (Eimers, 1999), while at the same time appreciating and connecting with the teaching knowledge that is inherent in that discipline (Trowler and Cooper, 2002).

Increasingly, educational development specialists understand their role as engaging in collaborative learning processes with colleagues from diverse disciplines who are pursuing individual and shared interest in their students' learning (Taylor, 2005). At its best, this collaboration is characterized by a three-way interaction among the "personal context" of practice, the "public context" of theory, and the "shared context" of a community of discourse about teaching and learning that gives rise to "the development of new practices and more developed theories" (Rowland, 1999, p. 312). Generating this development dynamic in the disciplines is likely to have the greatest impact on student learning (Knight and Trowler, 2000). It is also essential to fostering scholarly teaching (Richlin, 2001): systematic, critical examination of how learning in each discipline can be improved.

New Directions for Teaching and Learning, no. 122, Summer 2010 © Wiley Periodicals, Inc.
Published online in Wiley InterScience (www.interscience.wiley.com) • DOI: 10.1002/tl.398

Bringing these different ways of knowing about teaching and learning together challenges educational developers to know—in an active sense— the disciplines in which we collaborate. In our work with colleagues, it is not sufficient to "know about" a discipline. Rather, our practice requires that we "know in" that discipline by participating in shared problem solving, discussions, debates, and commitment to learning and teaching (Palmer, 1998). The need for awareness of disciplinary influences is reciprocal. Educational developers themselves come from diverse disciplinary backgrounds and carry their own assumptions about knowledge, teaching, and learning. If used intentionally, this knowledge can be an asset; if used tacitly, it can become a barrier. This chapter explores the nature of disciplinary expertise and how an understanding of the diversity of knowledge structures, processes, and cultures across disciplines can optimize educational development practice.

The Disciplines

Parker (2002) captured the spirit of academic disciplines when, in contrasting the meaning of the terms *subject* and *discipline*, she characterized a subject as having a well-developed knowledge base that can be articulated, taught, learned, and assessed, whereas "a discipline is a more complex structure: to be engaged in a discipline is to shape, and be shaped by the subject, to be part of a scholarly community, to engage with fellow students—to become 'disciplined'" (p. 374). Reflecting this sense of discipline as a discourse community, Swales (1990) contends that engagement in a discipline requires not only shared knowledge of a subject matter but also shared goals, methods of inquiry, and language and communication processes. To work effectively in the disciplines, educational developers do not need to become subject experts; we have our own expertise to bring to the collaboration. We do, however, need to appreciate (and work with) the goals, methods, communication styles, and cultures of different disciplines (Eimers, 1999; Green, 2008; Taylor, 2005).

Elements of Disciplinary Knowledge. Are there common elements of disciplinary knowledge that can frame our appreciation of a diverse spectrum of disciplines? A number of scholars have identified a common framework useful to understanding our work in the disciplines (Dressel and Marcus, 1982; Phenix, 1986; Lattuca and Stark, 2009):

- Substance (what do we know and what do we study?)
- Language and symbols (how do we express and communicate knowledge?)
- Modes of inquiry (what methods are used to identify questions and to collect, interpret, and judge evidence?)
- Organization (how do we organize knowledge within our discipline and in relation to other disciplines?)

NEW DIRECTIONS FOR TEACHING AND LEARNING • DOI: 10.1002/tl

- Values (what assumptions and values influence the knowledge we pursue and how we pursue it?)

Disciplines (and major groups of disciplines) vary in significant ways with respect to how they view the nature of knowledge and knowing with respect to these common elements (Becher and Trowler, 2001; Donald, 2002; Kolb, 1982; Neumann, 2001). It is critical that educational development specialists appreciate the diverse approaches to knowledge organization, problem solving, values, and communication that characterize various disciplines. This knowledge has a real impact on our capacity to assist colleagues in making these aspects of expert knowledge explicit in their teaching and to understand how we can best foster reciprocal integration of theoretical and practice-based knowledge about teaching and learning in the disciplines.

Disciplinary Structures. The work of scholar-teachers is profoundly influenced by their disciplinary expertise, starting with the broad goals held by faculty for student learning. For instance, faculty in fields such as counseling or nursing are more likely to design learning experiences that help students develop skills in facilitating interpersonal problem solving, in contrast to fields such as engineering or business that are more likely to emphasize specific work-related skills (Smart and Umbach, 2007). Similarly, the sciences were found to emphasize acquisition and application of particular facts, principles, and concepts, whereas social sciences and humanities focused on acquisition of a broad knowledge base, fostering critical and creative thinking, and personal development (Braxton, 1995; Donald, 2002; Hativa, 1995).

Perhaps the most obvious influence is the role of disciplinary knowledge in faculty selection of concepts and theories to teach in a course. However, disciplinary influences on content are also manifested in subtler ways. Donald (2002) demonstrated how the number of concepts taught in a course and the relationships between those concepts varies widely, with science courses characterized by a larger number of concepts that are more tightly connected than courses in social sciences or humanities. Donald's comprehensive analysis also revealed how organization of course information mirrors organization of knowledge in different discipline groups. In fields such as the hard sciences, where there is a strong agreement on a number of core concepts, theories, and methods of inquiry, the structured pattern is manifested in course designs. In contrast, the patterns of course content across social sciences or humanities tended to be more loosely structured, reflecting the nature of knowledge in those disciplines. These differences in the nature and structure of discipline knowledge are important variables to consider when educational developers work with colleagues in the disciplines to plan learning experiences at the course and program levels.

Disciplinary Processes

Thinking. A second essential dimension of disciplinary expertise is how we process, create, and communicate knowledge in a discipline. Perhaps the most comprehensive differences were claimed by Kuhn (1970), who theorized that ways of thinking, methods of inquiry, and standards of evidence and of interpreting that evidence varied significantly across disciplines. More recently, Donald presented extensive evidence of different ways of thinking (2002) and validation processes and truth criteria (1990) across disciplines. Smart and Umbach (2007) add further evidence to demonstrate that irrespective of institutional type "faculty members . . . structure their undergraduate courses in a manner that allows them to place greater emphasis on the development of student competencies with the distinctive norms and values of their respective academic environments" (p. 184). Learning activities chosen to help students develop this knowledge parallel academic work in the disciplines: labs in science, design projects in engineering, cases studies in management, and text analysis in the humanities. The criteria by which the outcomes of this work are evaluated are shaped by the ways of writing, thinking, and research that characterize the forms of discourse and evidence that are valued in the discipline (Donald, 2002). To optimize the impact of their work with colleagues in the disciplines, educational developers need to craft a synergy between generic approaches to planning learning experiences and the disciplinary processes of inquiry that shape how faculty engage students in thinking and learning and inform how they assess the work students produce through these processes (Donald, 2002; Lattuca and Stark, 2009).

Communication. With respect to writing—the expression of thinking—Green (2008) illustrates some of the challenges in how scholarly writing on teaching and learning is perceived by colleagues in other disciplines. He reminds the educational development community of the importance of the core element of "language and symbols"—how various disciplines communicate their knowledge—and how failure to recognize the unique aspects of our own disciplinary knowledge can exclude colleagues from other disciplines from our practice. Given the layers observed, it is important that educational development specialists acknowledge disciplinary differences when they communicate knowledge about teaching and learning, and in turn when they facilitate colleagues in explicitly integrating learning theory in how they conceptualize and practice their teaching.

Disciplinary Culture. A third dimension of disciplinary expertise is the cultural context in which academic work, including teaching, is produced. The work of individual scholars is conducted in academic communities that share in, build on, discuss, critically evaluate, value, and recognize the work of its members (Brew, 1999). Although institutions,

NEW DIRECTIONS FOR TEACHING AND LEARNING • DOI: 10.1002/tl

and in particular departments, contribute to the cultural influences experienced by academics, "How faculty think, work and interact are primarily circumscribed by disciplinary boundaries" (Frost and Jean, 2003, p. 120). Consequently, a number of researchers have characterized differences across disciplines in social and cultural terms (Biglan, 1973; Becher and Trowler, 2001; Holland, 1997; Skelton, 2005).

Three findings are particularly relevant to educational development practice. First is the predisposition of some disciplines to value certain kinds of approaches to teaching. For instance, there is a tendency for academics in the hard sciences (such as physics or biology) to report more teacher-focused approaches to teaching than colleagues in the humanities (such as history and literature) who report more student-centered approaches (Lindblom-Ylänne, Trigwell, Nevgi, and Ashwin, 2006; Lueddeke, 2003; Trigwell, 2002). As a result, the impact on scholarly work of a request that colleagues dedicate scarce time resources to developing student-centered approaches to teaching may be perceived differently according to the discipline. Second is differentiation in the inclination of colleagues across disciplines to collaborate in sharing, building, and applying their collective knowledge about teaching and learning. For example, academic communities in the hard sciences tend to be "competitive but gregarious" (Neumann, Parry, and Becher, 2002, p. 406) and to have multiple collaborators and coauthors, whereas in academic communities in the humanities "enquiry is typically a solitary pursuit" (p. 406). It is understandable that collaboration with educational developers will come more naturally to some groups than others. Third, the fit between the intended practical outcomes of academic work aimed at improving students' learning experiences may be more compatible with applied disciplines. Pure fields tend to value knowledge for its own sake; applied fields tend to focus on products or techniques based on that knowledge in fields grounded in the hard sciences such as engineering or on improved practice in fields situated in social sciences and humanities (Neumann, Parry, and Becher, 2002). A sensitivity to these cultural differences helps educational developers appreciate the nuanced ways in which our requests to collaborate in teaching and learning initiatives are interpreted in various disciplinary contexts.

Teaching and Learning Knowledge in the Disciplines. Ways of knowing about teaching and learning are not exclusive to disciplines that study teaching and learning. Within each discipline there is a body of knowledge about how learning and teaching in the discipline takes place which has been generated largely through teaching practice in that discipline. Working effectively in the disciplines requires educational developers to recognize the value of both practice-based and theoretical knowledge of teaching and learning, and where appropriate to foster a synergy between them.

What comprises the teaching and learning knowledge of professors in different disciplines? From a review of the empirical literature, Trigwell and Shale (2004) identified three major domains of knowledge: (1) knowledge, which includes knowledge of the discipline, knowledge of teaching and learning, conceptions of teaching and learning, and knowledge of context; (2) practice, which includes teaching, evaluation, reflection, communication, and learning; and (3) outcomes, which includes both student and teacher learning.

In an empirical study of exemplary teaching incidents, Hum (2009) identified a five-factor model of practical teaching knowledge: pedagogical knowledge, delivery and management, content knowledge, monitoring and reflection, and knowledge of students. These broad categories of teaching knowledge map closely onto dimensions of the knowledge base of K–12 teachers identified by Shulman (1987), suggesting that these general categories of knowledge cross both disciplines and teaching contexts.

Beyond the level of general categories of teaching and learning knowledge, disciplines have been characterized as having distinct "teaching and learning regimes" (Trowler and Cooper, 2002, p. 221). The dimensions of these regimes are:

- One's professional identity as a teacher, the product of the conception of self as a teacher and self in relation to others
- Power relations between students and teachers, and how the teaching and learning role relates to other power structures in the institution (for instance, control over curriculum change)
- "Codes of signification" (p. 228) that reflect the value with which the culture of the institution holds persons, disciplines, or roles
- Tacit assumptions about students, teaching and learning, and the learning environment
- "Rules of appropriateness" regarding such matters as "patterns of classroom interactions, assessment strategies, activities students are required/requested to engage in, the behaviors of lecturers" (p. 230)
- "Recurrent practices," "unreflective habitual routines" (p. 231) that are learned in a practice community
- "Discursive repertoires" (p. 232), how members of a discipline community communicate about and in teaching
- "Implicit theories of teaching and learning" (p. 235), or beliefs about how learning is best facilitated

These analyses of teaching and learning knowledge illustrate the complexity of educational development roles. As we collaborate with colleagues in developing courses and programs, in finding more effective ways to help students learn, or in providing feedback on their teaching, we need to appreciate the teaching and learning regimes in different disciplines and assess the compatibility of a particular regime with our personal expertise. We also need to develop the versatility to translate teaching and learning knowledge in teaching and learning regimes without being seen to "promulgate a rigid, preferred model" (Trowler and Cooper, 2002, p. 238). Perhaps most important, our work in the disciplines demands that we create intellectual space in our educational development practice for colleagues to critically examine and build on their own teaching and learning regimes.

The challenge in this work is that much of the knowledge represented in disciplinary teaching and learning regimes is implicit, and difficult for even disciplinary experts to articulate. The evolution of the scholarship of teaching and learning (Huber and Hutchings, 2005) promises to furnish a critical resource to sharing and building discipline-based knowledge about how students learn. Proliferation of this form of scholarship has the potential to make knowledge about teaching, and learning, in the disciplines more transparent to both professors and students (for example, Pace and Middendorf, 2004). The scholarship of teaching and learning also offers a new sphere of educational development practice in the disciplines, as we more frequently collaborate with colleagues to plan and implement inquiries into their students' learning—a sphere that demands deep understanding of the knowledge about teaching and learning that resides in the disciplines.

Conclusion

An examination of discipline-based knowledge influences on the postsecondary learning experience underlines the importance of discipline-based knowledge in how postsecondary teaching is conceptualized, designed, implemented, and assessed. Whether educational developers are discipline specialists or engage in work across disciplinary communities, the concept of "knowing in community" (Palmer, 1998) is a critical dimension of our work. Palmer's concept of knowing is deep and requires not only knowing about the disciplinary community in which we work but also sharing in the goals, challenges, resources, and problem solving with that community. It is through such collaborations that we come to understand how knowledge structures, processes, and cultures of the disciplines influence the diverse approaches taken to teaching in our academic communities. It is also through these collaborations that we create opportunities to share and build knowledge with colleagues in the context where our efforts will have the most impact: embedded in teaching and learning in a discipline.

References

Becher, T., and Trowler, P. R. *Academic Tribes and Territories* (2nd ed.). Buckingham, UK: Society for Research into Higher Education and Open University Press, 2001.

Biglan, A. "Relationships Between Subject Matter Characteristics and the Structure and Output of University Departments." *Journal of Applied Psychology,* 1973, 57, 204–213.

Braxton, J. M. "Disciplines with an Affinity for the Improvement of Undergraduate Education." In N. Hativa and M. Marincovich (eds.), *Disciplinary Differences in Teaching and Learning: Implications for Practice*. New Directions for Teaching and Learning, no. 64. San Francisco: Jossey-Bass, 1995.

Brew, A. "Research and Teaching: Changing Relationships in a Changing Context." *Studies in Higher Education*, 1999, *24*, 291–301.

Donald, J. G. "University Professors' Views of Knowledge and Validation Processes." *Journal of Educational Psychology*, 1990, *82*, 242–249.

Donald, J. G. *Learning to Think: Disciplinary Perspectives*. San Francisco: Jossey-Bass, 2002.

Dressel, P., and Marcus, D. *On Teaching and Learning in College*. San Francisco: Jossey-Bass, 1982.

Eimers, M. T. "Working with Faculty from Different Disciplines." *About Campus*, 1999, *4*(1), 18–24.

Frost, S. H., and Jean, P. M. "Bridging the Disciplines: Interdisciplinary Discourse and Faculty Scholarship. *Journal of Higher Education*, 2003, *74*, 119–149.

Green, D. "New Academics' Perceptions of the Language of Teaching and Learning: Identifying and Overcoming Linguistic Barriers." *International Journal for Academic Development*, 2008, *14*(1), 33–45.

Hativa, N. "What Is Taught in an Undergraduate Lecture? Differences Between a Matched Pair of Pure and Applied Sciences." In N. Hativa and M. Marincovich (eds.), *Disciplinary Differences in Teaching and Learning: Implications for Practice*. New Directions for Teaching and Learning, no. 64. San Francisco: Jossey-Bass, 1995.

Holland, J. L. *Making Vocational Choices: A Theory of Vocational Personalities and Work Environments* (3rd edition), Odessa, FL: Psychological Assessment Resources, 1997.

Huber, M. T., and Hutchings, P. *The Advancement of Learning: Building the Teaching Commons*. Menlo Park, Calif.: Carnegie Foundation for the Advancement of Teaching, 2005.

Hum, G. "Determining University Professors' Practical Teaching Knowledge Constructs in Exemplary Incidents of Teaching." Unpublished master's thesis, McGill University, Montreal, Quebec, Canada, 2009.

Knight, R. T., and Trowler, P. R. "Department-Level Cultures and the Improvement of Learning and Teaching." *Studies in Higher Education*, 2000, *25*(1), 169–183.

Kolb, D. A. "Learning Styles and Disciplinary Differences." In A. W. Chickering, *The Modern American College*. San Francisco: Jossey-Bass, 1982.

Kuhn, T. S. *The Structure of Scientific Revolutions* (2nd ed.). Chicago: University of Chicago Press, 1970.

Lattuca, L. R., and Stark, J. S. *Shaping the College Curriculum: Academic Plans in Context* (2nd ed.). San Francisco: Jossey-Bass, 2009.

Lindblom-Ylänne, S., Trigwell, K., Nevgi, A., and Ashwin, P. "How Approaches to Teaching Are Affected by Discipline and Teaching Context." *Studies in Higher Education*, 2006, *31*, 285–298.

Lueddeke, G. "Professionalising Teaching Practice in Higher Education: A Study of Disciplinary Variation and 'Teaching Scholarship.'" *Studies in Higher Education*, 2003, *28*, 213–228.

Neumann, R. "Disciplinary Differences and University Teaching." *Studies in Higher Education*, 2001, *26*, 135–146.

Neumann, R., Parry, S., and Becher, T. "Teaching and Learning in Their Disciplinary Contexts: A Conceptual Analysis." *Studies in Higher Education*, 2002, *27*, 405–417.

Pace, D., and Middendorf, J. (eds.). "Decoding the Disciplines: Helping Students Learn Disciplinary Ways of Thinking." In *New Directions for Teaching and Learning*, no. 98. San Francisco: Jossey-Bass, 2004.

Palmer, P. *The Courage to Teach*. San Francisco: Jossey-Bass, 1998.

Parker, J. "A New Disciplinarity: Communities of Knowledge, Learning and Practice. *Teaching in Higher Education*, 2002, *7*, 373–386.

Phenix, P. H. *Realms of Meaning: A Philosophy of the Curriculum for General Education.* New York: McGraw-Hill, 1986.

Richlin, L. "Scholarly Teaching and the Scholarship of Teaching." In C. Kreber (ed.), *Scholarship Revisited: Perspectives on the Scholarship of Teaching and Learning.* New Directions for Teaching and Learning, no. 86. San Francisco: Jossey-Bass, 2001.

Rowland, S. "The Role of Theory in a Pedagogical Model for Lecturers in Higher Education." *Studies in Higher Education*, 1999, *24*, 303–314.

Shulman, L. S. "Knowledge and Teaching: Foundations of the New Reform. *Harvard Educational Review*, 1987, *57*(1), 1–22.

Skelton, A. "The Contribution of Subject Disciplines." In A. Skelton, *Understanding Teaching Excellence in Higher Education: Towards a Critical Approach.* New York: Routledge, 2005.

Smart, J. C., and Umbach, P. D. "Faculty and Academic Environments: Using Holland's Theory to Explore the Differences in How Faculty Structure Undergraduate Courses." *Journal of College Student Development*, 2007, *48*(2), 183–195.

Swales, J. M. *Genre Analysis: English in Academic and Research Settings.* Cambridge, UK: Cambridge University Press, 1990.

Taylor, K. L. "Academic Development as Institutional Leadership: An Interplay of Person, Role, Strategy, and Institution." *International Journal for Academic Development*, 2005, *10*(1), 31–46.

Trigwell, K. "Approaches to Teaching Design Subjects: A Quantitative Analysis." *Art, Design and Communication in Higher Education*, 2002, *1*, 69–80.

Trigwell, K., and Shale, S. "Student Learning and the Scholarship of University Teaching." *Studies in Higher Education*, 2004, *29*, 523–536.

Trowler, P., and Cooper, A. "Teaching and Learning Regimes: Implicit Theories and Recurrent Practices in the Enhancement of Teaching and Learning Through Educational Development Programmes." *Higher Education Research and Development*, 2002, *21*, 221–240.

K. LYNN TAYLOR *is the director of the Center for Learning and Teaching at Dalhousie University in Halifax, Nova Scotia.*

NEW DIRECTIONS FOR TEACHING AND LEARNING • DOI: 10.1002/tl

6

As faculty developers become more central as leaders within the university, strengthening their change management skills becomes more important for their success. Kotter's model of change management may be a useful tool for developers for this endeavor.

Moving from the Periphery to the Center of the Academy: Faculty Developers as Leaders of Change

Debra Dawson, Joy Mighty, Judy Britnell

Faculty development units have been in existence in North American universities and colleges for more than forty years (Boice, 1989; Knapper and Piccinin, 1999; Knapper, 2003). The early faculty development units were typically led by a committee or a part-time director who focused on presenting teaching tips in short workshops (Boice, 1989). Over the years, the role of these centers gradually evolved as they became more established, with increased staff and resources moving slowly away from a teaching-tips approach to evidenced-based programs of faculty development (Fletcher and Patrick, 1998). There has also been a shift in the role of faculty developers, moving from working to support the teaching needs of individual faculty to meeting more multidimensional needs of faculty (Arreola, Aleamoni, and Theall, 2003; Sorcinelli, Austin, Eddy, and Beach, 2006). Centers now respond to such other faculty development issues as supporting the overall professional development needs of midcareer faculty and providing career counseling to faculty members. In addition to responding to development goals of individual faculty, the centers also started attending to organizational goals, such as training chairs and assisting administrators with addressing institutional problems and needs (Fletcher and Patrick, 1998).

According to Sorcinelli and her colleagues (2006), we have moved in higher education from the 1960s and the "age of the teacher" to the current

NEW DIRECTIONS FOR TEACHING AND LEARNING, no. 122, Summer 2010 © Wiley Periodicals, Inc.
Published online in Wiley InterScience (www.interscience.wiley.com) • DOI: 10.1002/tl.399

"age of the network." It is now more likely that faculty developers work with a diverse cross-section of individuals within the university, which may range from provosts, deans and directors, and faculty members to technology experts, instructional designers, campus planners, and graduate teaching assistants. This transition has shifted the role of the faculty developer from the periphery to the center of the institution. In their new role, faculty developers must act as change agents and therefore must be aware of and apply models of organizational change to their work if they are to be successful in their new role as change leaders (Taylor, 2005).

Havnes and Stensaker (2006) conducted research to examine the evolving roles of faculty development centers and suggest that in Europe there are several factors that have led to a shift in the role of developers to change agents. First, they cite the Bologna process (an agreement among member countries of the European Union to standardize certain aspects of postsecondary education) as influencing institutions to concentrate on teaching and learning. Second, quality assurance systems require universities to focus on how they can improve teaching. They suggest that universities now recognize they must be capable of change. To help make the changes needed for organizational success, institutions are increasingly looking to faculty developers. Similarly, in the United States, Fletcher and Patrick (1998) proposed that in higher education there is an increased focus on accountability and a need to shift the academic culture to one that is more student-focused than faculty-focused. They too believe that faculty developers have a unique role to play in managing these changes within the institution. This movement toward faculty developers as change leaders appears to be global. Taylor's research in Australia (2005) found that as a result of the quality assurance movement faculty developers are increasingly looked on as an essential resource for leading change within the academy.

Competencies of Faculty Developers

In fact, recent research by Dawson, Britnell, and Hitchcock (2010) identified change management as a key competency of directors of teaching and learning centers. The research focused on identifying specific competencies, abilities, experiences, and traits necessary for roles at three levels within a learning and teaching center: entry level, senior level, and director. The researchers used World Café as a forum to facilitate a collaborative and discussion-based research process and to gather data at four gatherings of faculty developers within Canada and the United States. The richness of the data collected at each session was used iteratively in that information gathered from one session was used to inform the next. Building knowledge in this way resulted in a matrix of competencies for the three levels identified above. It is anticipated that this research will be instrumental in helping to define more clearly faculty developers' role at the various stages of their career and used by centers as they seek to employ an appropriate mix of faculty developers to ensure sustainability and success within their institutions.

In every gathering of faculty developers, participants always saw facilitating change management as a key competency for the role of director. Furthermore, when faculty developers were asked to rank-order the ten competencies needed for the position of director, facilitating change management was number two. This represents a shift from past research (for example, Wright and Miller, 2000) that did not list change management as a skill or competency required of faculty developers.

Kotter's Model of Leading Change

As change agents, faculty developers can draw on several models of change to guide their actions. Diamond (2005) has suggested that the model espoused by John Kotter (1996) is a useful framework for faculty developers to consider as facilitators of change within the university. This model has been one of the most widely used by organizations throughout North America since Kotter's groundbreaking book *Leading Change* was published in 1996. In his model, he describes eight steps of the transformational process, insisting that no step can be skipped without disastrous results (although several steps may occur simultaneously). Drawing on his analyses of hundreds of successful and failed change efforts in a variety of organizations, Kotter further emphasizes the importance of leadership in driving the process. Before exploring how faculty developers can apply the Kotter model in their role as change agents, the next section summarizes the model (Figure 1).

According to Kotter (1996), the first step in the process (at the top of the figure) is to *establish a sense of urgency*. He maintains that without feeling there is a compelling reason for change, members of the organization are content to maintain the status quo. The next step involves *creating a guiding coalition* made up of individuals and units with the expertise and commitment necessary to advance the change initiative. Critical among the attributes of such a coalition is credibility within the organization. Opponents of the change will find it difficult to overcome the influence of a group of committed, reputable, and trustworthy supporters who have strong relationships with others across the organization.

The third step in the process is to *develop a vision and a strategy*. According to Kotter, a vision imparts direction and serves to motivate members of the organization to act. In addition, a vision helps give the guiding coalition a clear mandate and strategy, specific timelines, and relevant resources. It also allows continuous evaluation of the progress. However, identifying a vision is not enough. Kotter's fourth step is to *communicate the vision of change*. An important aspect of communicating the vision is the need for leaders to model it in their behavior, which should be

Figure 1. Kotter's Eight-Stage Process on Leading Change

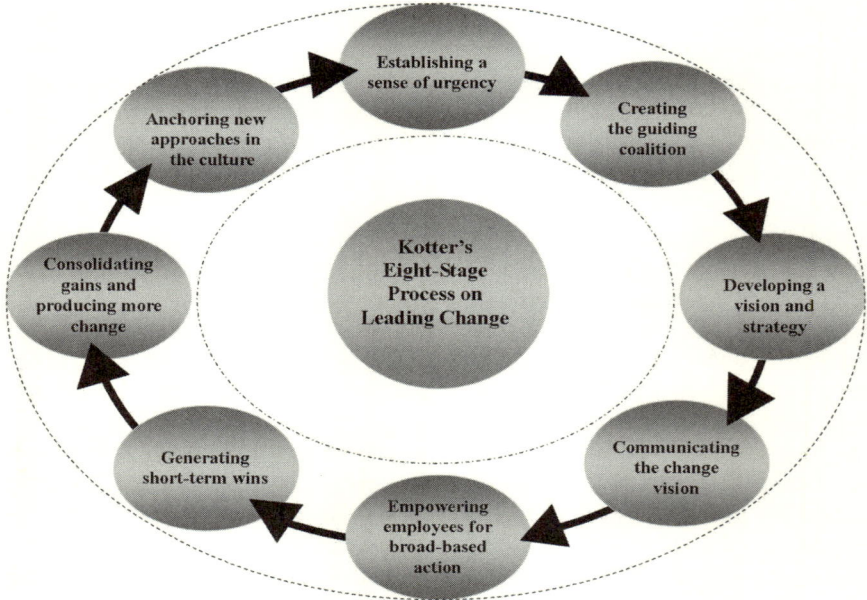

consistent with the words being articulated—a phenomenon known as "walking the talk." Failure to do so can severely undermine the change effort. The fifth step in Kotter's model requires the leaders of change to *empower for broad-based action.* This involves encouraging members of the guiding coalition to engage in creative problem solving to eliminate barriers and persist with the change process in spite of resistance. The change team should feel sufficiently safe to take risks in implementing the planned change.

The next step is to *plan for and create short-term wins,* or evidence of visible progress, to avoid losing momentum. Such wins, and the people who contribute to them, must also be recognized and rewarded. However, celebrations at this stage cannot be prolonged. The seventh step involves *consolidating the gains* made and using the increased credibility they afford in order to *produce more change.* Leaders must find ways of encouraging those involved in the change effort to persist in their efforts, rather than doing what Kotter calls declaring victory too soon. This necessitates establishing new milestones and involving additional groups to reinvigorate the process and diffuse the change. The final step in the model is to anchor the new approaches, or *institutionalize the change,* so that it is integrated into the organization's culture. According to Kotter, this involves explicitly articulating the connections between the improvements and the new approaches or behaviors.

Although Kotter's change model has been used primarily to explain change within business settings, one recent study demonstrated how it can have application to the university setting. Dwyer (2005) described how Kotter's model fit well with the process that was used at her college to overcome obstacles to changing the culture of assessment. For instance, a guiding coalition was created, called the Assessment Task Force. Determining how to empower broad-based action led the task force to provide funds to spur innovation. Short-term wins were highlighted in newsletters and speaker series. Consolidating gains came when the accreditation team commended their assessment efforts and reinforced the changes that had already occurred. In evaluating the change in the assessment process, it was evident that all eight of Kotter's steps had been completed. Kotter's model therefore has viability for facilitating change in the university culture. The model may be particularly useful in guiding the work of faculty developers in their role as change agents because it emphasizes that you do not need to be the manager to lead change. Regardless of their position in the formal organizational structure, faculty developers in their expanded role function as leaders to effect change. The next section describes two examples of how faculty developers are currently using Kotter's model to affect change in Canada.

Example One: Fostering Change Institutionally. At one large research-intensive university, there was an ongoing realization within the faculty development center that, although there had been general discussion about the need for more student engagement in experiential learning activities, discussion had been fairly localized. As a result, student opportunities to participate in experiential learning activities were limited to only a couple of programs rather than being systematically embedded within the entire curriculum. When the faculty development unit was invited to give a presentation to a strategic task force on student learning, it seized the opportunity to advocate for a more systematic approach to fostering experiential education on campus. In particular, the developer wished to facilitate integration of service learning into the curriculum. Change was going to occur as a result of a new strategic plan, but it was up to the faculty developer to demonstrate how blocks to curriculum innovation could be overcome, to make salient current obstacles, and to explain new language and terms to facilitate the change process. Clearly, one challenge to this change was budgetary restrictions, which promoted use of large-class teaching and movement away from faculty-student contact (an essential component of student engagement).

The results of the National Survey of Student Engagement were used as observable and concrete evidence that the students on campus were seldom engaged in experiential education activities, and used to create *a sense of urgency*. There were those who saw student engagement initiatives such as service learning and community-based research as devaluing education by watering down the curriculum (challenge). The strategic task force was already in place (*the guiding coalition*), so the major task was to help shape the vision and be able to communicate that vision successfully. Faculty champions were brought to the task force to support the initiative and furnish concrete examples of student engagement initiatives in the classroom. As Kotter suggests, it is important to create an imaginable *vision of the future*. Showcasing local faculty innovators highlighted that this vision of the future was attainable. This was vital to the success of the project. The final strategic plan strongly focused on enhancing student engagement.

Next steps in the project involved creating opportunities for faculty to learn about experiential education activities; the faculty development center held several conferences and used an existing committee to keep promoting and reinforcing new ideas for student engagement (*communicating the vision*). In addition to empowering faculty for broad-based action, these activities also allowed the centers to highlight *short-term successes* in implementing this new approach to teaching. Kotter reminds us that, to *consolidate change and make more gains*, leaders must keep the purpose of the vision apparent to all, bring in more resources when necessary, and recognize that consolidating change can be a lengthy process. Anchoring new approaches in the culture is the final step of Kotter's model. Clearly, in this case changing the practice of teaching to a far more learner-centered approach is challenging because it requires a shift in culture and the institution is not yet in that final phase. For this to be successful, it is essential that the faculty developer see herself as a change leader within the organization and look for opportunities to overcome the gaps between the desired state, which in this case was the development of a curriculum that valued student engagement, and the current state, which only offered limited opportunities for engagement to students in specific programs. Our role as developers is to reduce barriers, grasp opportunities as they arise, and keep nurturing the vision.

Example Two: Fostering Change Beyond the University. The second example illustrates how Kotter's model can be used by faculty developers to influence change outside their institution. In 2005, growing concern about the quality of postsecondary education in the province of Ontario led the Council of Ontario Universities (COU, the organization of executive heads of Ontario's publicly assisted universities) to establish a task force made up of members of one of its subgroups, the Ontario Council of Academic Vice-Presidents (OCAV), to develop guidelines for university "undergraduate degree level expectations" (UDLEs). These guidelines were meant to serve as a framework for describing expectations of attributes and performance by graduates of all universities in Ontario (OCAV, 2007).

There were numerous reasons for articulating the UDLEs. They were in part a response to expressions of concern about the quality of postsecondary education and calls for accountability from governments, employers, students, and society in general. More important, the COU and OCAV

NEW DIRECTIONS FOR TEACHING AND LEARNING • DOI: 10.1002/tl

sought to encourage curriculum renewal. It was hoped that, as degree-level outcomes, the UDLEs would help to guide curriculum development and supply criteria for assessing achievement of educational objectives. They further hoped that institutions would align their courses and programs with these provincewide expectations, thereby supporting transparency and authenticity, ensuring quality, and ultimately enhancing students' educational experience and learning. In addition, the degree-level expectations were seen as consistent with both the international quality assurance movement and the trend toward standardization of degree structures and expectations.

Having developed the degree-level outcomes, the COU and OCAV were faced with the challenge of influencing universities across the province to adopt them. It was at this point that the COU and OCAV sought the assistance of the instructional developers of Ontario (now called the Council of Ontario Educational Developers or COED). The developers recognized this was a watershed moment for faculty development in Ontario and a great opportunity to influence curriculum change at the course, program, and institutional levels. It was an opportunity for leading significant systemwide change. OCAV and COED established a Joint Working Group on Teaching and Learning to identify strategic approaches for assisting universities in incorporating the degree-level outcomes framework into their curricula. This group became the *guiding coalition* for the proposed changes. The working group met over several months to plan for this change initiative. To create *a sense of urgency,* the working group had to identify and communicate compelling reasons for institutions to change. Several such reasons were identified, among them the need for our graduates to be able to compete nationally, accreditation issues, and particularly pressures for greater accountability in postsecondary education in the province. One of the most compelling reasons was to satisfy the COU requirement that by June 2008 universities would develop policies for incorporating the degree-level competencies into the undergraduate program review processes to which all member universities subscribed. Building on the OCAV documents, the working group sought *to develop a vision and strategy* for change. Again, Kotter (1996) suggests that several steps may occur simultaneously, so long as no step is skipped.

Having identified several compelling reasons for universities to adopt the UDLEs, the working group developed a strategy for communicating this urgent need for change and *to communicate the vision.* They planned a series of regional workshops for faculty developers and academic leaders, each to be facilitated by two faculty developers and an academic vice president (*to empower employees for broad-based change*). An important objective of each workshop was to build capacity for incorporating the UDLEs in the institution's curricular review process, thereby moving curricular reform forward (this serves to *anchor new approaches in the culture and helped consolidate gains and produce more change*).

NEW DIRECTIONS FOR TEACHING AND LEARNING • DOI: 10.1002/tl

This example demonstrates how a group of faculty developers used Kotter's model to help bring about systemwide curricular change in one geographic region. As Kotter suggests, change is often a slow process and leaders need to be prepared to ensure each step is successfully completed before moving on to the next. Some *short-term wins* have been created as all member institutions begin adopting use of the UDLEs in the curriculum review process. The next steps will be to consolidate gains and anchor the changes in the culture. The role of faculty developers as change agents is critical to the success of this project.

Implications for the Future of Faculty Development

These examples demonstrate that Kotter's model can be a rich resource for helping developers guide change at their institution and beyond. However, the model has some limitations because it was designed for a more corporate setting. For instance, within universities there is frequent turnover in the senior administration that may have a significant impact on implementation of new initiatives and require the developer to seek buy-in more than once. Second, although the role of the developer is shifting more to the center of the institution, few developers have senior administrative posts, which may limit their ability to lead change or even effectively communicate the change vision within the university. Their powers of persuasion will be tested in leading change in such complex organizations. Although Dawson, Britnell, and Hitchcock's research (2010) found that change management was a critical competency of directors, this may not be one that developers feel as knowledgeable about as they do about their competencies in other domains. In fact, in her survey of 560 developers Chism (2007) found that on entry to their profession they rated their knowledge of organizational change as very low. Given how critical change management is for faculty developers' success at the senior career level, this suggests that more must be done to help developers acquire this competency at an earlier stage of their career.

In addition to developing competencies in change management, as Taylor (2005) and Winer and Weston (2009) suggest, we may need to reconceptualize how we use our time as faculty developers. In the past, our work has often focused on working one-on-one with faculty members and sharing teaching tips for success (Boice, 1989). Although this one-off work was generally successful, it was unlikely to lead to the systemic change necessary to transform the teaching culture within the institution. Fletcher and Patrick (1998) also suggested that the work of faculty developers must shift from holding workshops for individuals to a broader role as change agent within the institution. Recently, Winer and Weston (2009) stated that the outcome of our work must move from the micro (individual) level to at least the macro level where we influence the institutional approach to teaching and learning. At this level, faculty developers are far more involved in influencing policies and shifting the teaching culture. An example of this would be work on facilitating integration of service learning and other experiential opportunities into the strategic plan of one university. The final level our work may move to is the mega level, where our influence extends to the field or beyond the institution. This is illustrated by the guiding coalition involving the faculty developers who led the UDLEs project. This is a dramatic change in the work of faculty developers. Winer and Weston propose a template for centers to assess their current work and suggest the importance of targeting increases in work at the macro and mega levels if faculty development units are to be seen as central to their institution's mission. Faculty developers seem poised to take on a seminal role in the transformation of the university, given their strong skills in communication, team building, and collaboration (Dawson, Britnell, and Hitchcock, 2010).

References

Arreola, R. A., Aleamoni, L. M., and Theall, M. *Beyond Scholarship: Recognizing the Multiple Roles of the Professoriate*. Paper presented at American Educational Research Association (AERA) Convention, Chicago, April 2003.

Boice, R. "Psychologists as Faculty Developers." *Professional Psychology: Research and Practice*, 1989, *20*(2), 97–104.

Chism, N. V. N. *A Professional Priority: Preparing Future Developers*. Paper presented at the 32nd Annual Meeting of the Professional and Organizational Development Network in Higher Education (POD), Oct. 2007, Pittsburgh.

Dawson, D., Britnell, J., and Hitchcock, A. "Developing Competency Models of Faculty Developers: Using World Café to Foster Dialogue." *To Improve the Academy*, 2010, *28*, 3–24.

Diamond, R. M. "The Institutional Change Agency: The Expanding Role of Academic Support Centers." *To Improve the Academy*, 2005, *23*, 24–37.

Dwyer, P. M. "Leading Change: Creating a Culture of Assessment." *To Improve the Academy*, 2005, *23*, 38–46.

Fletcher, J. J., and Patrick, S. K. "Not Just Workshops Anymore: The Role of Faculty Development in Reframing Academic Priorities." *International Journal for Academic Development*, 1998, *3*(1), 39–46.

Havnes, A., and Stensaker, B. "Educational Development Centers: From Educational to Organizational Development?" *Quality Assurance in Education*, 2006, *14*(1), 7–20.

Knapper, C. "Three Decades of Educational Development." *International Journal for Academic Development*, 2003, *8*(1, 2), 5–9.

Knapper, C., and Piccinin, S. "Consulting About Teaching: An Overview." *New Directions for Teaching and Learning*, no. 79. San Francisco: Jossey-Bass, 1999.

Kotter, J. P. *Leading Change*. Boston: Harvard Business Press, 1996.

Ontario Council of Academic Vice-Presidents (OCAV). "Guidelines for University Undergraduate Degree Level Expectations," 2007. Retrieved [December 12, 2009] from www.lib.uwo.ca/files/teaching/OCAV_UDLE.pdf.

Sorcinelli, M. D., Austin, A., Eddy, P. L., and Beach, A. L. *Creating the Future of Faculty Development: Learning from the Past, Understanding the Present*. Bolton, Mass.: Anker, 2006.

Taylor, K. L. "Academic Development as Institutional Leadership: An Interplay of Person, Role, Strategy, and Institution." *International Journal for Academic Development*, 2005, *10*(1), 31–46.

Winer, L., and Weston, C. *Reconsidering the Impact of Educational Development Work.* Paper presented at the Educational Developers Caucus Conference (EDC), Oshawa, Ont., February 2009.

Wright, A., and Miller, J. "The Educational Developer's Portfolio." *International Journal for Academic Development,* 2000, 5(1), 20–29.

DEBRA DAWSON *is the director of Teaching and Learning Services at the University of Western Ontario. Her work as an educational developer has spanned more than twenty years and allowed her to pursue her passion for adult learning. Her current research interests are in the areas of student engagement and educational development.*

JOY MIGHTY *is the director of the Center for Teaching and Learning, and a professor in the School of Business, at Queen's University. Her special interests are organizational development and change, as well as equity and diversity issues as they relate to both management and education.*

JUDY BRITNELL *is the director of the Learning and Teaching Office at Ryerson University. She is committed as an educational developer to contribute to her university's mission of a high-quality educational experience for all students.*

SECTION THREE

Reflections

The scholarship of teaching and learning is highlighted within this chapter as one approach for educational developers to use in examining the impact of their practice at a programmatic and institutional level.

Assessing the Impact of Educational Development Through the Lens of the Scholarship of Teaching and Learning

Carolyn Hoessler, Judy Britnell, Denise Stockley

Within this chapter, we convey what scholarship of teaching and learning is and is not, and how educational developers can and do engage in such scholarship to grow as individual providers, units, and academic institutions seeking to continue improving teaching and learning. Further, the advancement of effective teaching techniques, expansion of theory on student learning, and the growth of teaching assistant and instructor training call for continuous scholarship as a key facet of educational development. Scholarship of teaching and learning (SoTL) is the litmus test for identifying and sharing the educational development practices that have an impact on teaching and student learning. In addition, by engaging instructors and administration in SoTL, educational developers can support the advancement of teaching at their institution. The resulting SoTL constitutes a shared foundation of effective practices and theory for educational developers to draw on as informed consultants and general idea connectors.

Defining

Based on several proposed definitions and descriptions, SoTL is an integrated aspect of academic scholarship that goes beyond great and informed teaching (Boyer, 1990; Kreber, 2002; Richlin, 2001). Boyer's scholarship

(1990) blurs prior distinctions among basic research, interdisciplinary research, applied research, and teaching by positing the deeply intertwined and responsive nature of "four separate, yet overlapping functions" (p. 16) of scholarship, addressing:

What is there to know? (scholarship of discovery)
What does it mean? (scholarship of integration)
How could it be useful? (scholarship of application)
How to build students' understanding of it? (scholarship of teaching)

Research and Publication as Key Components of Scholarship

Recent scholars, such as Richlin (2001), make the distinction between scholarship about teaching and teaching based on scholarship. She defines *scholarly teaching* as improvement of teaching practices through research that supports student learning in one's own course, whereas *scholarship of teaching* involves formal peer-reviewed dissemination to share findings with the wider scholarly discussion on teaching and learning.

Other theorists further split teaching into three segments. Kreber and Cranton (2000) proposed three forms of knowledge: instructional (how-to) knowledge, pedagogical knowledge (of theory and research), and curricular knowledge (of the program and course goals), encompassing content reflection, process reflection, and premise reflection. Kreber (2002) further proposes three teaching concepts:

Teaching excellence: Successful and effective performance, as perceived by students, peers, and oneself, requires sound understanding of the topic and of how to convey that knowledge to students on the basis of personal experience, literature, or research.
Teaching expertise: Informed mastery involves development of pedagogical content knowledge (that is, how to teach and what to teach) through continuous forethought, controlled performance, and self-reflection. Through this process, experts become even more effective; thus expert teachers are excellent teachers, though not all excellent teachers are experts.
Scholarship of teaching: Scholars link theory with practice (connecting skills and broader theory) through participation in conferences, peer-reviewed publications, mentoring, and discussions. This final level strengthens teaching excellence and expertise; in addition, the larger academic community on teaching is advanced.

Reflection, a component of Kreber and Cranton's forms of knowledge (2000), appears to be incorporated into all three concepts of Kreber (2002). Thus great, informed, and researched teaching all involves reflection on one's own teaching and research.

Scholarship of teaching and learning by educational developers and instructors contributes to excellence in teaching and scholarly teaching by building a foundation of theory-based and rigorously tested techniques that educational developers and university instructors can use. Beyond the classroom, scholarship of teaching and learning can also inform and examine educational development practices.

In Action

Scholarship of teaching and learning encompasses research on discipline-specific and cross-discipline theoretical frameworks and methods for advancement of teaching and learning. Educational developers play a dual role, encouraging and supporting SoTL at their institution as well as engaging in SoTL in their own initiatives. The aim of scholarship of teaching and learning is to find out what works and why; by testing approaches to see what has an impact, the quality of teaching and learning is advanced. Recognizing and rewarding instructors' scholarship of teaching and learning an evidence-based scholarship index was found by Brew and Ginns (2008) to be significantly related to improvements in overall student course experience (and specifically good teaching, clear goals and standards, and generic skills of university teachers). Their scholarship index, developed at the University of Sydney, is a set of weighted and scored criteria defining four components of SoTL: teaching excellence, incorporation of educational research in teaching (akin to scholarly teaching), publishing or presenting SoTL research, and reflection as part of teaching and learning courses.

Measuring the Impact of Our Educational Development Practices

Educational developers are involved in a range of courses, programs, consultations, and other initiatives, which are highlighted within the chapters in this book. Although the impact of our work may be seen in the conversations and reported changes that follow, engaging in SoTL is important for informing our work and demonstrating its effectiveness to others. As with any research, SoTL involves learning from existing literature, rigorously testing our own practices, studying the potential influences and demonstrable impacts, and disseminating the findings beyond one's home context to the larger scholarly community. Workshops, consultations, programs, and other initiatives form the basis of educational developers' daily work. Often evaluated on the basis of usage or satisfaction with limited past research on effectiveness, there is a growing need to determine whether these practices have an impact on teaching and student learning through research and SoTL (for example, Brew, 2002; Kreber and Brook, 2001; Marincovich, Prostko, and Stout, 1998; Weimer and Lenze, 1991). Ideally, measuring impact should be incorporated as new programs are planned or existing programs are reviewed—for example, conducting a needs assessment, which may include interviews, focus groups, and questionnaires.

In the past decade, SoTL has contributed to understanding the impact of several educational development practices. Workshops on teaching were found by Rust (1998) to successfully affect teachers' reported practice. In addition, participants' plans at the end of the workshop to make change did predict later changes in their practice. Piccinin, Crishi, and McCoy (1999) examined the impact of various forms of consultation on teaching as measured by student ratings and found that brief consultations regarding feedback showed improvement one to three years later. When these consultations also included class observation by itself or in combination with student consultation, the results were an immediate improvement by the end of the semester that was sustained one to three years later when reassessed. SoTL also indicates long-term impact (two years later) of a novice training program on teaching practices (based on self-report), although there was a contextually dependent effect on institution-level changes (Stes, Clement, and Van Petegem, 2007). Sustained change is important; it is not only current but future teaching that educational developers seek to improve, and demonstrating such impact is an important responsibility of educational developers who plan and implement practices.

To facilitate evaluation of programs, several scholars have developed processes for educational development and higher education in general and some offer examples of measuring impact. Kreber and Brook (2001) present a guide to evaluating the impact of educational development programs that considers key process questions such as when, why, who, and how to evaluate; it encompasses approaches that are tied to foci of evaluation such as teaching performance, student learning, and beliefs about teaching and learning. A framework by McAlpine and Harris (2002) includes the language needed to develop clear and criteria-based standards for evaluating teaching practice. In addition, Gray and Radloff (2008) have explored conceptualizations of impact and its effect on educational development outcomes and motivations.

Looking Closely at an Example within Educational Development Units

Scholarship can inform individual practice, course development, and initiatives, and it can also serve to support the growth of educational development units. SoTL can strengthen and renew models of operation to improve the effectiveness and sustainability of educational development centers by informing decisions and evaluation of existing units on the basis of shared research, theory, and examples of best practice.

Taking a scholarly approach, an example illustrates how Kotter's model (1996, as described in the chapter by Dawson, Mighty, and Britnell in this volume) can be used to facilitate change within an educational development center itself. A center within a large urban university is the focus of this example; it was established in the early 1970s, but a series of budget decisions contributed to erratic development over the seventies and eighties. In the 1990s, the center received some formal funding that enabled establishment of a part-time director and some educational development programming. Right after 2000 several changes contributed to establishing the *sense of urgency* or major opportunity that Kotter (1996) purports is essential to a successful change process. These changes included a dramatic increase in the hiring of new full-time faculty, which led to greater demand for faculty development activities; the spearheading of a program review by the co-director of the center during her sabbatical (Schönwetter, Dawson, and Britnell, 2009); and a vice provost who gave full support to reviewing the mandate and function of the center. Because this institution had received university status in 1993, there was also a perceived need to balance a focus on teaching with concomitant growth in research and graduate studies. It was evident that the status quo would not be well suited to changing faculty and the development of the university.

Faculty and staff who were committed to teaching were gathered from across the university to form the *guiding coalition*. Many of the individuals were experienced teachers and some were teaching award recipients, possessing high credibility as teaching leaders within their schools and departments. Others in the coalition had made major contributions to the development of the center over the years. A highly regarded external consultant, well known in educational development circles, was also a key contributor to this group. The mandate of the coalition was clear: to conduct a program review of the center and make recommendations to the Academic Council (Senate), the guiding academic body of the university.

The outcome of the program review of the center took the form of twenty-two recommendations, which gained the full support of the Academic Council (*creating a vision*). The vice provost, who had commissioned the review, responded to the recommendations and with his guidance and support the recommendations were implemented. The director of the center also met directly with the deans and directors across the university, communicating this new model of educational development to them (*communicating the vision*).

The model that was developed in 2003 corresponds to a model cited by Rotheram (2005) in which a network of faculty members is jointly responsible to the center and also to their own faculty. These faculty associates act as direct consultants to their own faculties and also organize or catalyze the activities of others to foster teaching development. The new model gained the interest and support of deans and directors, and subsequently collaborative interviews and selection of these individuals took place in each faculty. This momentum required the support of administrators and ultimately the interest of faculty to occupy these new positions. The faculty associate position was not without risks; it involved adoption

NEW DIRECTIONS FOR TEACHING AND LEARNING • DOI: 10.1002/tl

of a new role and was a steep learning curve for the new faculty associates (*empowering others to act on the vision*). One faculty member chose to delay the selection until the following year, so there was some flexibility in the evolution of the new model.

The role of each faculty associate was to lead a teaching-focused initiative in his or her respective faculty that would promote the professional development of others. As well, they would work with the center to promote a universitywide professional development opportunity. Over the years, faculty development programs such as a teaching-for-success series and an orientation program specifically designed for part-time instructors were implemented. These programs were well publicized and recognized across the university for their focus on contributions to teaching quality enhancement. New programs of educational development were offered to faculty, for example instructional skills workshops and a new university teaching development program. These programs were also well publicized, and where appropriate, participants' successes were publicly celebrated (*planning for and creating short-term wins*).

The model has been successful to varying degrees in each of the faculties such that some revisions and redevelopment of the model have recently been undertaken (*consolidating improvements and producing still more change*). A revised model that combines the efforts of a strong central educational development center with new teaching leadership roles in the faculties is being proposed. Building the teaching leadership capacity of faculty members in the local faculties is a major focus of this new model. New change agents in the form of teaching chairs, school- and department-level "champions" in teaching, and teaching action groups will all contribute to a positive focus on teaching and teaching improvements (see the chapters by Lewis and by Fraser, Gosling, and Sorcinelli within this volume for additional models).

Following Kotter's change model, the final step is to make certain that the mission of the educational development center is aligned closely and clearly with the university's academic plan (*institutionalizing new approaches*). The newly revised model has been presented to the academic planning group of the university several times to ensure clarity of the model, and it has their full support. As the new model is implemented, it will be important to revisit aspects of Kotter's change theory to ensure that the changes being proposed are well communicated and that once under way the short-term wins are publicized and rewarded.

Meeting the Challenge of Recognizing Scholarship of Teaching and Learning

The role of educational developers as proponents and supporters of teaching within academic institutions suggests a third level for engaging in scholarship of teaching and learning as well as promotion of such

New Directions for Teaching and Learning • DOI: 10.1002/tl

scholarship. As indicated by this case, administrative leaders, departments, and faculties shape the extent to which teaching and work to improve teaching is recognized and rewarded. SoTL can inform development of criteria and policies to support engagement in both teaching and scholarship.

One of the first hurdles to recognizing scholarship is tied to the discussion on defining SoTL. To shift general perceptions of scholarship of teaching from just "good teaching" requires policy changes; many academic staff do not share the view that scholarship of teaching is more than just effective teaching (Kreber, 2003). Engaging administrators and faculties in developing criteria that define and substantiate how scholarship is a unique contribution lays a foundation for policy change. Smith (2001) suggests formative evaluations of good teaching, scholarly teaching, and teaching scholarship are needed to advance all three areas proposed by Kreber (2002). Developing evidence-based criteria for teaching excellence, scholarly teaching, and scholarship of teaching and learning involves performance-based indicators:

Components	Evidence
Teaching excellence	Student-experience evaluations and awards
Consideration of existing educational research	Inclusion and application of research in own teaching (for example, textbooks)
Reflection on own teaching and own research about teaching	Engagement in accredited courses on teaching and learning in higher education
Research on teaching and learning	Publishing and presenting the findings

In Brew and Ginns's (2008) study, scholarship of teaching and learning (as conceptualized by Kreber and Cranton, 2000) was matched with a measurable set of criteria as part of their Scholarship Index to recognize and reward the scholarly community. Thus existing scholarship is a foundation for informing development of criteria for recognizing and rewarding scholarship of teaching and learning at academic institutions.

Conclusion

In summary, engagement in scholarship of teaching and learning involves research into the process and outcomes of teaching and learning, including examining the effectiveness of educational development practices. SoTL can inform as well as result from reviews of educational development units and the development of evidence-based criteria recognizing teaching and learning. Educational developers can contribute to SoTL across their multiple roles involving creation and coordination of training programs, consultation with individual instructors, engagement in educational development units, and leadership in institutional policies. The take-home

NEW DIRECTIONS FOR TEACHING AND LEARNING • DOI: 10.1002/tl

message of this chapter is that there is existing work to inform and inspire, and a great need to engage in and support scholarship of teaching and learning. Continued improvement and growth as educational developers, as a field, and as academic leaders fosters teaching excellence and scholarly teaching and contributes to the knowledge base that supports our footsteps.

References

Boyer, E. L. *Scholarship Reconsidered: Priorities of the Professoriate*. Princeton, N.J.: Carnegie Foundation for the Advancement of Teaching, 1990.

Brew, A. "Research and the Academic Developer: A New Agenda." *International Journal of Academic Development*, 2002, 7(2), 112–122.

Brew, A., and Ginns, P. "The Relationship Between Engagement in the Scholarship of Teaching and Learning and Students' Course Experiences." *Assessment and Evaluation in Higher Education*, 2008, 33(5), 535–545.

Gray, K., & Radloff, A. The idea of impact and its implications for academic development work. *International Journal for Academic Development*, 2008, 13(2), 97–106.

Kotter, J. P. *Leading Change*. Boston: Harvard Business Press, 1996.

Kreber, C. "Teaching Excellence, Teaching Expertise, and the Scholarship of Teaching." *Innovative Higher Education*, 2002, 27(1), 5–23.

Kreber, C. "The Scholarship of Teaching: A Comparison of Conceptions Held by Experts and Regular Academic Staff." *Higher Education*, 2003, 46, 93–121.

Kreber, C., and Brook, P. "Impact Evaluation of Educational Development Programmes." *International Journal for Academic Development*, 2001, 6(2), 96–108.

Kreber, C., and Cranton, P. A. "Exploring the Scholarship of Teaching." *Journal of Higher Education*, 2000, 71(4), 476–495.

Marincovich, M., Prostko, J., and Stout, F. (eds.). *The Professional Development of Graduate Teaching Assistants*. Bolton, Mass.: Anker, 1998.

McAlpine, L., and Harris, R. "Evaluating Teaching Effectiveness and Teaching Improvement: A Language for Institutional Policies and Academic Development Practices." *International Journal for Academic Development*, 2002, 7(1), 7–17.

Piccinin, S., Crishi, C., and McCoy, M. "The Impact of Individual Consultation on Student Ratings of Teaching." *International Journal for Academic Development*, 1999, 4(2), 75–88.

Richlin, L. "Scholarly Teaching and the Scholarship of Teaching." In C. Kreber (ed.), *Revisiting Scholarship: Perspectives on the Scholarship of Teaching*. New Directions for Teaching and Learning, no. 86. San Francisco: Jossey-Bass, 2001.

Rotheram, B. "Institutional Commitment to Learning and Teaching Centers." Paper from 2005 International Forum of Teacher Scholars, 2005. Retrieved from http://www.stlhe.ca/en/stlhe/constituencies/3m/pdf/Bob%20Rotheram.pdf

Rust, C. "The Impact of Educational Development Workshops on Teachers' Practice." *International Journal for Academic Development*, 1998, 3(1), 72–80.

Schönwetter, D., Dawson, D. L., and Britnell, J. "Program Assessments: Success Strategies from Three Canadian Teaching Centers." *Innovative Higher Education*, 2009, 33(4), 239–255.

Smith, R. "Expertise in Teaching and in the Scholarship of Teaching." In C. Kreber (ed.), *Revisiting Scholarship: Perspectives on the Scholarship of Teaching*. New Directions for Teaching and Learning, no. 86. San Francisco: Jossey-Bass, 2001.

Stes, A., Clement, M., and Van Petegem, P. "The Effectiveness of a Faculty Training Programme: Long-Term and Institutional Impact." *International Journal for Academic Development*, 2007, 12(2), 99–109.

Weimer, M., and Lenze, L. F. "Instructional Interventions: A Review of the Literature on Efforts to Improve Instruction." In J. C. Smart (ed.), *Higher Education: Handbook of Theory and Research*. New York: Agathon Press, 1991.

CAROLYN HOESSLER is the graduate student coordinator for the Center for Teaching and Learning, Queen's University. Her research interests encompass the social, interpersonal, and motivational influences shaping educational and professional development experiences.

JUDY BRITNELL directs the Learning and Teaching Office at Ryerson University. She is committed as an educational developer to contribute to her university's mission of a high-quality educational experience for all students.

DENISE STOCKLEY is associate director of the Center for Teaching and Learning at Queen's University. Her research focus is on pathways to the profession of education development, educational technology, and graduate supervision.

NEW DIRECTIONS FOR TEACHING AND LEARNING • DOI: 10.1002/tl

8

Educational development is driven by strong value commitments, and yet there are questions concerning the key goals that educational development strives to achieve.

Value Commitments and Ambivalence in Educational Development

David Gosling

The concept of development is a value-loaded term. In whatever context it is used—child development or economic development, for example—the term *development* implies something more than simply change. It implies moving toward an approved goal, toward something that is valued. So to understand educational development we need to explore what is valued by developers as individuals and as an emerging community of practice.

But educational development is a diverse field and this diversity is reflected in the range of value commitments held by individual developers. It is precisely because the goals of educational development are to some degree contested that "our notions of development are of necessity a site for encounter and dispute" (Webb, 1996, p. 65). Nevertheless, there are some clear areas of agreement, which have been neatly summarized by Clegg (2009): "Educational development is a project committed to improvement and innovation, and one imbued with strong value commitments to students, their learning and the quality of teaching" (p. 409).

This chapter looks at what we understand by "values" and then at the values that motivate individuals to become (and remain) educational developers. It also considers the values adopted in some national educational development networks as a way of interrogating the collective values of this diverse community of practice. Finally we look at some of the difficulties that arise when these values come into conflict with the increasingly dominant managerial culture of universities today.

NEW DIRECTIONS FOR TEACHING AND LEARNING, no. 122, Summer 2010 © Wiley Periodicals, Inc.
Published online in Wiley InterScience (www.interscience.wiley.com) • DOI: 10.1002/tl.401

Values

Values are central to human behavior. They motivate us to act and they are the basis of the judgments we make about our own and others' behavior in both the private and public spheres. Dewey (1916, p. 249) distinguishes between valuing as "the attitude of prizing a thing, finding it worthwhile, for its own sake or intrinsically" and "a distinctively intellectual act—an operation of comparing and judging." He notes that in the first sense values are virtually synonymous with the aims of education. This is because the values we hold reflect what we think is important and what we believe is in our interest. They may be things that we value for their own sake—beauty, integrity, truth—or they may be things we believe are instrumental in achievement of intrinsic goods.

However intrinsic and instrumental values are not always easy to distinguish. Student learning—acquisition of knowledge, skills, attitudes, and capabilities—may be understood as an instrumental good, that is, as a means to achieve a better career, for example; or it may be regarded as intrinsically good, "simply the cultivation of the intellect, as such, and its object is nothing more or less than intellectual excellence" (Newman, 1976, originally published 1853, p. 121).

There is a difference between the activities we prioritize as being important and valuable, such as student learning, and the values that inform the end goals of this learning. There is considerable agreement about what educational development values as important activities, such as teaching and learning, using learning technologies, and fair assessment of students; but there is less agreement (and there has been less debate about) the goals of these activities. By avoiding the debate about what educational development is ultimately aiming for, developers have given themselves greater flexibility in working with university managers, but, I shall argue, they have left a question mark over the key goals they are striving to achieve.

Values Held in Common

Central to educational development is the belief that teaching is important. Stated in this way, this seems to be an unremarkable value. Many would agree with Parker Palmer (1998) that "teaching and learning are critical to our individual and collective survival and to the quality of our lives" (p. 3), but the significance of this value can be understood only within the wider context of universities as they have developed over the last forty years or so. As Dill (2005) has argued, when universities apply pressure on academics to generate income or to raise the ranking position of the department and the institution, and individuals seek to gain promotion and increase their earning potential, "faculty members will choose to limit their time investment in teaching and to maximise their time investment in graduate instruction and research" (p. 181).

It is only against the background of the priority given to research, generating income, and publications, particularly in research-led universities, that the insistence on the value of teaching comes fully into focus. It is Boyer (1990) who has been most influential in making the argument that "other forms of scholarship—teaching, integration and application—must be fully acknowledged and placed on a more equal footing with discovery" (p. 75). Boyer's plea for the value of teaching as a form of scholarship has resonated strongly with educational developers throughout the world, not least because many have been driven by a *moral imperative* to improve teaching.

This is clear when developers talk about what motivated them to become interested in teaching. Here, "Roy" (fictional name) describes his own experience of being a student. He reports that one set of lectures consisted of the lecturer simply reading from his book, and "each week, like idiots, we wrote it all down."

> That fuse, being melodramatic, lit at that point . . . , and it's still there. I still hate, get angry about, bad teaching, and bad course design, and lousy assessment. I'm afraid there's a lot, and I'm glad there's a lot, still to be angry about. It keeps me working.

Roy was one of the relatively early pioneers of educational development in the United Kingdom, interviewed as part of a project to explore the histories of educational development (Gosling and Clegg, 2010; Grant and others, 2009). He reveals, in this quote, his commitment to values about what is good and bad teaching, about the need to change university teaching, and about the perceived personal responsibility of individuals such as himself to bring about that change.

Closely linked to the value placed on good teaching has been the goal to improve student learning. Sometimes educational development has appeared to proceed on the assumption that if teaching is improved, including course design, assessment, and using learning technologies, then students' learning will be improved. But improving student learning has also become highly rated as a value in its own right and is perhaps what matters most to educational developers, as this statement suggests:

> There are common values and what mattered most to people were things like—well, profoundly, a preoccupation with student learning. And a view of students as being the real clients or beneficiaries of our work, a notion of pedagogic progress (that it's always possible to do things better) and that what we are striving to do is improve our thinking and practice around the pedagogic function [Land, 2004, p. 194].

Deeply held values have a material effect on professional lives. Most educational and faculty developers have, at some point in their career, been required to make choices where they have prioritized development of teaching over other possible career paths. Mary Huber (2004) has charted such decisions in her account of the careers of four Carnegie Scholars. Dan Bernstein's choice to put "the teaching stuff first" by prioritizing development of peer review at Nebraska over being an editor of a discipline journal is one example of a choice that not only was a value commitment but also involved a "change of identity" (p. 55). Such choices can be highly risky and sometimes put promotion in doubt (Huber, 2004, p. 13), though in other cases there can be congruence between values and career opportunities (Gosling, McDonald, and Stockley, 2007).

Although there is no doubt that educational development involves a strong commitment to improving teaching and student learning, there is another value that also drives many developers. This is the commitment to support individual academics and all those involved in supporting learning in higher education and to care about their well-being. As one interview respondent in the United Kingdom critical histories project (Gosling and Clegg, 2010) declared, "I am passionate about people fulfilling their potential," and as another said about educational development, "It's individually oriented." This value is most clearly seen when the developer takes on "the facilitator role of somebody who helps you and talks to you" even when this means "subverting" institutional goals. This value relates to the strand that has been called the "personal" or "counseling" orientation of educational development (Boud and Macdonald, 1981). See Fraser, Gosling, and Sorcinelli's chapter in this volume for additional information.

Another value that is worth mentioning is educational development's support for innovation. What Land (2004) has described as a "modernist project," educational development has championed "the new" over tradition. It has valued change, and "change processes" based on "evidence-based practice," as a form of progress toward a more enlightened tertiary education. The new "science" of pedagogy was intended to shine a light on the ignorance and dogmatism that had characterized university life previously. Academic development set about replacing pedagogical superstition (about, for example, the value of lectures or examinations) with modern ways of achieving "effective learning." Academic developers have seen themselves as pioneering, revolutionary, overcoming the old forces of order that were based on class, privilege, and established hierarchies (Lee, Manathunga, and Kandlbinder, 2008). Innovation has become one of the key values of educational development.

Values of the Community of Practice of Educational Development

The values that educational development networks proclaim in their constitution are reifications of individual values, in the sense that they take on a reality of their own as guiding principles providing continuity and a focus for joint activity (Wenger, 1998).

So what are the values that educational development networks commit to? In the case of the Staff and Educational Development Association (SEDA, United Kingdom), they are:

- An understanding of how people learn
- Scholarship, professionalism, and ethical practice
- Working in and developing learning communities
- Working effectively with diversity and promoting inclusivity
- Continued reflection on professional practice
- Development of people and processes [Staff and Educational Development Association, Core Mission and Values; http://www.seda.ac.uk/about.html]

The Professional and Organisational Development (POD) Network in Higher Education (United States) summarizes its value commitments this way:

> POD believes that people have value, as individuals and as members of groups. The development of students is a fundamental purpose of higher education and requires for its success effective advising, teaching, leadership, and management. Central to POD's philosophy is lifelong, holistic, personal, and professional learning, growth, and change for the higher education community [About POD Network, http://www.podnetwork.org/about.htm]

In both networks, these brief statements of values allow individual members of the networks to interpret them in their own way. Nevertheless, some key words do receive elaboration. POD elaborates on the commitment to personal well-being by saying that:

> This includes wellness management, interpersonal skills, stress and time management, assertiveness development and a host of other programs which address the individual's well-being [Faculty Development: Definitions, http://www.podnetwork.org/faculty_development/definitions.htm]

In SEDA's case, for example, the value "scholarship, professionalism and ethical practice" is elaborated as follows:

> Staff and educational developers should develop, and pass on to their clients, a questioning and analytical approach, and the appropriate theoretical tools to continue to improve their practice within an ethically-based context [Professional Development: Fellowship and Associate Fellowship, http://www.seda.ac.uk/fellowships.html]

As a value, however, this is not specifically characteristic of educational development but might be regarded as a definition of academic scholarship. It might also be argued that the notion of an undefined "ethical context" is highly problematic if, as Barnett has argued, universities are a "site of value freedom" (Barnett, 2000, p. 111).

Despite this lack of clarity, applicants for SEDA Fellowships have to demonstrate through submission of appropriate evidence "commitment to the underpinning SEDA values." SEDA Fellowships are awards of professional accreditation for those involved in academic staff and educational development within the postcompulsory education sector both in the United Kingdom and internationally. Assessors of the award have to pass judgment on whether fellowship candidates are committed to SEDA values. Assessors are warned to "pay particular attention to any material presented within the portfolio or during the interview that might reasonably be felt to go against the SEDA values" (SEDA, Fellowship Handbook, p. 38; http://www.seda.ac.uk/resources/files/fellowshiphandbook.pdf.).

Through the mechanism of evaluating would-be Fellows' portfolios, SEDA acts as a gatekeeper and judge. In doing so SEDA passes judgment not only on the applicants' professional standing but also on their value commitments.

Another value found in the networks' statements relates to "diversity." SEDA talks about "working effectively with diversity and promoting inclusivity," which is defined as

> the recognition that each person has their own learning needs, and brings their own knowledge, characteristics and resources to the learning process [Fellowship Outcomes, paragraph 4, http://www.seda.ac.uk/fellowships.html].

It is noticeable that *diversity* is defined with respect to different "learning needs" that do not require any specific commitment to specific political goals such as antiracism or feminism. Nor does the guidance help when developers are faced with the difficulties of supporting diversity. Should diversity be supported when students from countries where women have a lower status than men treat a female lecturer with contempt, or when student attitudes toward homosexuality contradict a commitment to diversity of sexual orientation? General statements about the value of diversity tend to be silent on how to deal with such difficulties in multiculturalism.

The environment in which the Higher Education Learning and Teaching Association of South Africa (HELTASA) works is particularly sensitive to the post-Apartheid political context. The core values of HELTASA are

> Collegiality; professionalism; quality; equity; excellence; development; creativity; criticality; innovation [HELTASA, Mission and Vision, http://associated.sun.ac.za/heltasa/vision.html].

Of these core values, "equity" stands out as being a more overtly political value than any other, although the full implications of supporting the principle of equity are not spelled out. Given the broader political context, it is perhaps surprising that a recent study of academic development units in South Africa revealed that explicitly political goals were mentioned in the mission statements of only two units (Gosling, 2009).

All the (English-speaking) educational development networks identify the importance of collaboration or collegiality as a value, although it is expressed in different ways. The (Canadian) Educational Developers Caucus (EDC) within the Society for Teaching and Learning in Higher Education (STLHE), for example, has three aims, which all relate to collegiality in some way. The caucus aims to:

- Create a national forum where emerging and problematic educational development issues can be candidly discussed
- Create a collegial network within which information, strategies, and resources can be shared
- Facilitate communication among educational developers who are members of STLHE [Educational Developers Caucus, ByLaw Aims, http://www.stlhe.ca/en/stlhe/constituencies/edc/index.php]

At one level, these are aims that might be found in any organization and embody values that are internal to the practice of supporting any network or community of practice. The significance of these statements as values is revealed in the behavior of the members. Are they actually willing to candidly discuss issues that are problematic? Are they actually willing to share resources? What priority do they give to communicating with other educational developers?

Statements of values both create and reflect what one person has called "a like-mindedness" (Land, 2004, p. 194). Within the community of educational developers, working collaboratively seems to be an area of "like-mindedness" that guides and informs the behavior of individuals in a real way, as Yvonne (a pseudonym) testifies:

> The national community has been unbelievably supportive. And I look at colleagues with a traditional discipline like history and think "Blimey, I don't suppose they get very much support from the history discipline when things are going badly in their institution." But you know, I could lift the phone and talk to anybody and I do think, partly because we're a much smaller community, we were very close in those days, so there was an awful lot of mutual support of people who at that one point happened to be under fire in their own institution [Gosling and Clegg, 2010].

Another developer talked about "the spirit of collegiality that characterizes the educational development field," which meant colleagues "encouraged our work and perhaps even more significantly, formed the beginning of a network of colleagues that would grow into a critical asset in my career" (participant in the Pathways Project; see Gosling, McDonald, and Stockley, 2007). Another faculty developer, also a participant in the Pathways Project, talking about POD, said:

> What I have learned and relearned all along the way is that POD has been, is, and, always will be dedicated to creating a professional space that is generative, renewing, based on discourse across boundaries, and offering mutual support, collegiality, and community in every sense of those words.

The value of collaboration not only characterizes how educational developers seek to work together; it also informs how they work with academic colleagues: "My instincts and everything I had done thus far told me that I needed to be consultative, responsive, and collaborative rather than prescriptive" (participant in the Pathways Project). Furthermore, the commitment to values is seen by members as an important part of the glue that holds networks together: "SEDA's strengths are, two things, one its commitment to be collaborative, and the other is its ability to be flexible but retain its values" (K. Mason-O'Connor of Cheltenham and Gloucester College, personal communication, August 2009).

Some Problems with Values in Educational Development

In view of everything that has been said so far, it is surprising that much of the discourse of educational development is at first glance values-free. In the educational development literature we commonly find expressions such as "effective learning," "enhancing learning," "quality learning," "teaching excellence," "critical analysis," "reflective practice," and "effective teaching strategies." For example, the aim of one university's initial professional development course in the United Kingdom—and this is typical—is to enhance the "effectiveness" of teaching:

> To enable staff to develop the knowledge and skills to enhance the effectiveness of their current teaching and assessment practice and to support the practice of others [Postgraduate Certificate in Learning and Teaching in Higher Education, Content and Structure, Module 1; http://www.liv.ac.uk/eddev/teaching_qualifications/PG_Cert/Content_Structure.htm].

Another example, this time from the United States, presents the argument for "preparing future faculty" in terms of "today's need for faculty who are not only able researchers but also effective teachers and leaders of their profession" (Gaff, Pruitt-Logan, and Webl, 2000, p. 5). "Effective" teachers have qualities such as "a serious commitment to teaching," "strong communication skills," and "willingness to engage in a great deal of social interaction" (Gaff, Pruitt-Logan, and Webl, 2000, p. 45), but at no point does the publication elucidate what ends effective teaching might have. Only in a section on "developing the capacity to teach diverse students" is there a specific value commitment to "teaching methods that reflect genuine respect for and understanding of the heterogeneous mix of students that populate higher education" (p. 60).

The use of the word *effective* should ring an alarm bell. MacIntyre described "effectiveness" as "among the central moral fictions of the age" (1981, p. 71). It is a term well loved by managers who "conceive of themselves as morally neutral characters whose skills enable them to devise the most efficient means of achieving whatever end is proposed" (p. 71). But effectiveness only masquerades as a morally neutral concept.

First of all, the term "effective (and also "excellence") is often used to hide value commitments. What counts as "effective learning," and "excellence in teaching," is relative to the goals of the learning and teaching practice (Skelton, 2004). So effective learning for graduates to become entrepreneurs will be very different from effective learning for students to become academic researchers.

Second, despite appearing to be uncontentious, effectiveness is not necessarily the most important educational value. There may be other considerations more important than being effective: respecting autonomy, encouraging freedom, supporting ethical behavior. It is not obvious, and it should not be taken for granted, that effective learning is more important than achieving these other values if they are in conflict.

Educational development has come into being in a period when the influence of political liberalism is at its height. Rawls has been at the forefront of arguing that it is not the place of public institutions to "presuppose accepting any particular comprehensive religious, philosophical, or moral doctrine: rather the political conception presents itself as a reasonable conception for the basic structure alone" (Rawls, 1996, p. 175). This means that no particular conception of what is right, what constitutes human fulfilment, or what would make for a better world should intrude into public life. Instead, the "basic structure" of public institutions should focus only on removing barriers to individuals' "equal opportunity to advance any conception of the good" (p. 192).

Since educational development came into being during this recent period with political liberalism at its most influential, it reflects a wider set of assumptions about tertiary education in being strong on the value of processes such as "learning" but reluctant to commit itself on what learning is valuable for. There is a commitment to raising the status of teaching as a professional activity, but there is less discussion about what the goals of teaching should be (Walker, 2002). There is value placed on good course design, through constructive alignment, for example (Biggs, 2003), without questioning what the goals of the curriculum should be. The assumption seems to be that it is not the role of faculty developers to determine these goals; they are determined by the academic teachers in specific programs or by the management of the institution. But educational development is actually only reflecting a deeper embarrassment about values that has resulted in universities as well as outside private and religious foundations maintaining silence over values (Barnett, 2003).

But some have argued that the goals of teaching and learning, and the scholarship of teaching, should be made more explicit. Kreber has argued, for example, that a "critical perspective on the scholarship of teaching" would challenge us "to explore the extent to which our teaching practice contributes to social justice education" (Kreber, 2005, p. 401). The challenge is a more general one, not simply to educational developers but to the academy as a whole. How does the academy respond to the questions put by David Orr (1990, as cited by Kreber, 2005, p. 397)?

> In a time of global turmoil, what transcendent purposes will this ideal academy serve? In a time of great wrongs, what injustices will it right? In an age of senseless violence, what civil disorders and dangers will it resolve? In a time of anomie and purposelessness, what higher qualities of mind and character will it cultivate?

Without a clear position on these questions, educational development departments can find themselves serving the goals of others even when these goals may not be compatible with the values of individual developers. Universities around the globe are increasingly understood as market-oriented, with students as "customers" and research output as a commodity. Universities have succumbed to managerialism (Bergquist, 1992) and to "academic capitalism" (Slaughter and Leslie, 1997). In this environment, academic work is seen as "the management of student learning" (Henkel, 2005) and educational development as having institutional responsibility for ensuring "delivery" of institutional goals by target setting, policy development, and surveillance of academic behavior through quality enhancement measures such as audit and peer review. This has led to the accusation that educational development "is dependent on and implicated in those very managerial practices from which some practitioners wish to distance themselves. Moreover, some developers enthusiastically embrace these powers" (Clegg, 2008, p. 5).

The Challenge Facing Educational Development

The question that haunts educational development at the present time is whether the institutional positioning of educational development, serving the goals set by their institutions, is compatible with the integrity of individual developers. The values that are closest to the hearts of developers, notably the value of teaching and improvement of student learning, are in danger of being expropriated by the demands of marketing and income generation. The discourse of the "student experience," which conceives of students as customers and higher education as a product, is replacing the language of learning and teaching. Educational developers face the dilemma of whether to be complicit in this reconceptualization of the university or to resist it (remaining true to their values) and risk marginalization. This dilemma is creating, for some at least, professional "identity schisms" (Winter, 2009), which remain unresolved at the present time (Lee and McWilliam, 2008).

References

Barnett, R. *Realizing the University in an Age of Supercomplexity*. Buckingham, UK: Society for Research in Higher Education and Open University, 2000.

Barnett, R. *Beyond All Reason: Living with Ideology in the University*. Buckingham, UK: Society for Research in Higher Education and Open University Press, 2003.

Bergquist, W. H. *The Four Cultures of the Academy*. San Francisco: Jossey-Bass, 1992.

Biggs, J. *Teaching for Quality Learning at University: What the Student Does* (2nd ed.). Buckingham, UK: Society for Research in Higher Education and Open University Press, 2003.

Boud, D., and Macdonald, R. *Educational Development Through Consultancy*. Guildford, UK: Society for Research in Higher Education, 1981.

Boyer, E. *Scholarship Reconsidered: Priorities of the Professoriate*. New Jersey: Princeton, 1990.

Clegg, S. *Forms of Knowing and Academic Practice*. Paper presented at Higher Education Close-Up 4, University of Cape Town, South Africa, 2008.

Clegg, S. "Forms of Knowing and Academic Development Practice." *Studies in Higher Education*, 2009, 34(4), 403–416.

Dewey, J. *Education and Democracy*. London: Macmillan, 1916.

Dill, D. D. "The Degradation of the Academic Ethic: Teaching, Research and the Renewal of Professional Self-Regulation." In R. Barnett (ed.), *Reshaping the University: New Relationships Between Research, Scholarship and Teaching*. Maidenhead, UK: Open University Press, McGraw-Hill Education, 2005.

Gaff, J. G., Pruitt-Logan, A. S., and Webl, R. A. *Building the Faculty We Need*. Washington, D.C.: Association of American Colleges and Universities and the Council of Graduate Schools, 2000.

Gosling, D. "Survey of Directors of Academic Development in South African Universities." HELTASA, 2009, Retrieved [August 2009] from http://associated.sun.ac.za/.

Gosling, D., and Clegg, S. "Critical Histories of Academic Development in the United Kingdom" (ongoing research project). Leeds Metropolitan University, 2010.

Gosling, D., McDonald, J., and Stockley, D. "We Did It Our Way! Narratives of Pathways to the Profession of Educational Development." *Educational Developments*, 2007, 8(4), 1–6.

Grant, B., Lee, A., Clegg, S., Manathunga, C., Barrow, P., Kandlbinder, P., Brailsford, I., Gosling, D., and Hicks, M. "Why History? Why Now? Multiple Accounts of the Emergence of Academic Development." *International Journal for Academic Development*, 2009, 14(1), 83–86.

Henkel, M. "Academic Identity and Autonomy in a Changing Policy Environment." *Higher Education*, 2005, 49, 155–176.

Huber, M. T. *Balancing Acts: The Scholarship of Teaching and Learning in Academic Careers*. Washington, D.C.: American Association for Higher Education, 2004.

Kreber, C. "Charting a Critical Course on the Scholarship of University Teaching Movement." *Studies in Higher Education*, 2005, *30*(4), 389–405.

Land, R. *Educational Development: Discourse, Identity and Practice*. Maidenhead, UK: Open University Press, McGraw-Hill, 2004.

Lee, A., Manathunga, C., and Kandlbinder, P. (eds.). *Making a Place: An Oral History of Academic Development in Australia*. Milperra, N.S.W.: Higher Education Research and Development Society of Australasia (HERDSA), 2008.

Lee, A., and McWilliam, E. "What Game Are We In? Living with Academic Development." *International Journal for Academic Development*, 2008, *13*(1), 67–77.

MacIntyre, A. *After Virtue*. London: Duckworth, 1981.

Newman, J. H. *The Idea of a University*. Oxford: Oxford University Press, 1976. (Originally published 1853)

Orr, D. W. "The Liberal Arts, the Campus and the Biosphere." *Harvard Educational Review*, 1990, *60*(2), 205–217.

Palmer, P. J. *The Courage to Teach*. San Francisco: Jossey-Bass, 1998.

Rawls, J. *Political Liberalism*. New York: Columbia University Press, 1996.

Skelton, A. "Understanding 'Teaching Excellence' in Higher Education: A Critical Evaluation of the National Teaching Fellowships Scheme." *Studies in Higher Education*, 2004, *29*(4), 451–468.

Slaughter, S., and Leslie, L. L. *Academic Capitalism: Politics and the Entrepreneurial University*. Baltimore, Md.: Johns Hopkins University Press, 1997.

Walker, M. "Pedagogy and the Politics and Purposes of Higher Education." *Arts and Humanities in Higher Education*, 2002, *1*(1), 43–58.

Webb, G. "Theories of Staff Development: Development and Understanding." *International Journal for Academic Development*, 1996, *1*(1), 63–69.

Wenger, E. *Communities of Practice: Learning, Meaning and Identity*. Cambridge, Mass.: Cambridge University Press, 1998.

Winter, R. "Academic Manager or Managed Academic? Academic Identity Schisms in Higher Education." *Journal of Higher Education Policy and Management*, 2009, *31*(2), 121–131.

DAVID GOSLING is a Visiting Research Fellow at the University of Plymouth, United Kingdom. He was head of educational development at the University of East London and is now an international higher education researcher, currently working on a critical history of educational development in the United Kingdom.

NEW DIRECTIONS FOR TEACHING AND LEARNING • DOI: 10.1002/tl

9

*Despite the evolution and increasing maturity of the field
of faculty development over the last five decades, it currently
lacks diversity of social identities and perspectives.*

Unheard Voices Among Faculty Developers

Joy Mighty, Mathew L. Ouellett, Christine A. Stanley

If we look at the current literature and practice of faculty development through various lenses, one thing remains clear: there are voices that are missing from the discourse. Whether viewed from the perspective of our separate pathways into the profession (our backgrounds, disciplinary contexts, or career progression) or from the perspective of leadership, politics, values, or theory, the conclusion remains the same: there is much work to be done to harness the diverse unheard voices among faculty developers in the field. In this chapter, we define *unheard voices* as those who are still on the margins of the profession—faculty developers who are diverse in terms of age, race, ethnicity, nationality, cultural identity, religious and spiritual identity, sexual orientation, social and economic status, gender identity, physical and mental ability, political ideologies and perspectives, and other dimensions of social identity. We include among the unheard the voices of faculty developers who reside and practice the profession in developing countries. We also include voices that are unheard because they are not being voiced, as well as those that are voiced but are not heard because others (particularly those in positions of power and influence) may not be prepared to hear them.

As past presidents of the Professional and Organizational Development (POD) Network in Higher Education (USA) and the Society for Teaching and Learning in Higher Education (STLHE) in Canada, we acknowledge that our perspective on the subject of unheard voices in the profession may have a North American bias. In addition, as we reflect on our experiences

NEW DIRECTIONS FOR TEACHING AND LEARNING, no. 122, Summer 2010 © Wiley Periodicals, Inc.
Published online in Wiley InterScience (www.interscience.wiley.com) • DOI: 10.1002/tl.402

as leaders in POD and STLHE, we recognize that these organizations have several characteristics in common. Both have the mutual vision of advancing excellence in teaching and learning, and both have espoused a commitment to valuing diversity and inclusivity, and to ensuring that they mirror the increasing diversity and internationalization of the population of their home country and beyond.

When we look at POD and STLHE as examples of organizations that value diversity, we notice that the demographics of their membership have changed tremendously since these organizations were founded in 1975 and 1981, respectively. However, even though there is diversity in terms of members' pathways into the profession and disciplinary contexts, some would argue that we need more sustained and focused attention on the diversity of voices that make up our membership in general and the field of faculty development in particular. Faculty developers represent an array of multiple social and cultural identities, and they often come to the profession seeking ways to broaden the canon, so that ultimately the work we do in faculty development will enhance the teaching and learning dialogue at our institutions, especially as it relates to diversity and social justice.

Changing demographics have clear implications for the future of many higher education institutions (Johnson and Lollar, 2004). One implication is that diversity should become central in our efforts to foster excellence in teaching and learning. Incorporating diversity in teaching and learning necessitates faculty developers taking a hard look at a variety of factors, including the "pipeline." A pipeline is a system through which something is conducted, especially as a means of supply. To be responsive to the increasing diversity in higher education, the field of faculty development needs to monitor the supply of future faculty developers to ensure that it is representative of diverse voices. This requires paying attention to past and future career development practices, and the hiring and staffing of teaching and learning centers.

One of the authors recently interviewed a purposive sample of fifteen North American faculty developers to conduct an exploratory, qualitative study of the pipeline for faculty developers. The participants were diverse in terms of discipline, number of years in the field, leadership experiences in faculty development organizations (nationally and internationally), institutional contexts, and multiple social and cultural identities. Among the questions asked was, "Where do you see voids in the pipeline for diversity among faculty developers?" Participants identified several areas, but eight are relevant to the issues raised in this chapter about unheard voices:

Leadership at the organizational level
Leadership when staffing teaching and learning centers
Learning from faculty developers from marginalized groups about their experiences in the field

NEW DIRECTIONS FOR TEACHING AND LEARNING • DOI: 10.1002/tl

Working collaboratively with historically black colleges and universities (HBCUs), Native American tribal colleges (NATC), and Hispanic-serving institutions (HSIs)

Mentoring

Supporting and mentoring individuals when they are in the field

Socialization in the field

Interdisciplinary points of entry into the field

It was evident from these conversations that listening to, learning from, and integrating the perspectives of unheard voices are ways to ensure that there is a pipeline of diverse faculty developers in the field.

A review of the faculty development literature over the past twenty years reveals tremendous strides taken to address diversity issues in teaching and learning, and in particular faculty development. However, the literature is fairly scant regarding pipeline issues for diversity in the profession (Stanley, 2001). Even more telling is that the arguments made by administrators and faculty developers across higher education institutions for valuing diversity and globalization have not always kept pace with the diversity of unheard voices among faculty developers in the field. Therefore, a logical and critical place to begin to address this is to work deeply and broadly to capitalize on the diversity of voices among faculty developers.

The Missing Voices

The field of faculty development in North America reflects the broader landscape of much of higher education; generally, it is a mostly white community (Henry and Tator, 2009). Several attempts have been made to be more inclusive of minority groups. For example, in the United States in the late 1990s POD established a diversity committee within its governance structure. This committee has sought to create and sustain a pipeline of diverse faculty development practitioners by sponsoring two initiatives, the Travel Grant Program and the Internship Program. Both of these programs are structured around models of mentoring and require a significant degree of commitment and participation (Ouellett and Stanley, 2004; Stanley, 2001). Launched in 1995, the POD Mentoring Program has also been somewhat successful in introducing a more diverse group of people to the field of faculty development and in supporting their success as practitioners. Awardees of these programs have made important contributions to the scope of activities and programs at POD annual conferences, and they have brought important insight into the experiences of faculty and academic administrators of color across all types of institutions (Ouellett and Stanley, 2004). They have cited the positive mentoring and network of collegial relationships they developed as the most important and rewarding aspects of their internships. Also, interns reported that the opportunity to work closely with directors, faculty, and staff in the host centers for teaching and learning contributed importantly to the success of their internship experience. Collectively, directors reported that their centers and institutions derived high-quality materials produced by the interns, new relationships with different faculty members, and stronger ties with a more diverse cohort of future staff and faculty members.

The clearest organizational success story in bringing a more diverse voice to the field of faculty development is the Historically Black Colleges and Universities Faculty Development Network, founded in 1994. Historically black colleges and universities (HBCUs) have a unique tradition, culture, and mission in the context of higher education in the United States. The HBCU Network has been instrumental in facilitating institutionalization of educational development at HBCUs, as well as in highlighting the innovations in teaching and learning taking place at these institutions (Dawkins, Beach, and Rozman, 2006). The POD and HBCU Networks reflect the national historical landscape across the United States, a predominantly white institution (PWI) and a much smaller, parallel organization for institutions serving HBCUs, historically Spanish institutions (HSI), and tribal colleges. Despite initiatives such as the examples described above, however, the voices of members of First Nations, other racial and ethnic minorities, and those from developing countries remain at a critically low level in the field.

Challenges of Including Missing Voices

It is relatively easy to acknowledge that there are voices missing from the discourse on faculty development. Much more challenging is the task of redressing the balance. There are several reasons for the current exclusion or underrepresentation of some social identity groups not only from faculty development but from postsecondary institutions in general. Chief among these reasons is the history of exclusion perpetuated by power holders in political, economic, and social organizations, including educational institutions. The legacies of colonialism, slavery, and hegemony, in which dominant social identity groups oppressed and excluded minority groups along with former slaves and their offspring, are still evident in many of the social systems and institutions of the twenty-first century, despite progress made in some areas such as the legal system and to a lesser extent in politics. Thus the tradition of exclusion persists, in part out of habit, even in institutions of higher education and their professional associations that espouse the values of equity and diversity. In other cases, some voices have remained silent by choice, almost in protest against the status quo and what are often perceived as token efforts to include them. Finally, some voices have remained unheard because of enduring assumptions of homogeneity, despite differences in social identity. Yet it is clear that the experiences and perspectives of social identity groups in our

NEW DIRECTIONS FOR TEACHING AND LEARNING • DOI: 10.1002/tl

institutions as well as in our faculty development organizations differ significantly.

Such exclusion is rarely intentional. Peggy McIntosh's classic work (1988) on how she came to understand white privilege and male privilege is instructional here. As McIntosh explains, in trying to understand why the men in her institution were resisting establishment of a women's studies program, she realized that their resistance stemmed from the unearned privilege they had received by having their issues and their views treated as the taken-for-granted norms. That was just the way it had always been, and for these men it was inconceivable that anyone would want to change the status quo. McIntosh had an epiphany when she realized that her whiteness had afforded her similar privileges relative to her female colleagues of color. In her words:

> As a white person, I realized I had been taught about racism as something which puts others at a disadvantage, but had been taught not to see one of its corollary aspects, white privilege, which puts me at an advantage. . . . I have come to see white privilege as an invisible package of unearned assets which I can count on cashing in each day, but about which I was "meant" to remain oblivious. White privilege is like an invisible weightless knapsack of special provisions, assurances, tools, maps, guides, codebooks, passports, visas, clothes, compass, emergency gear, and blank checks (McIntosh, 1988, p 1).

After McIntosh's epiphany, she realized that her new awareness made her responsible for acting to change the status quo; she could no longer ignore what she now knew to be true.

> Describing white privilege makes one newly accountable. As we in women's studies work to reveal male privilege and ask men to give up some of their power, so one who writes about having white privilege must ask, "Having described it, what will I do to lessen or end it?" (McIntosh, 1988, p. 1).

The examples and lessons from McIntosh pertain to gender, color, and race, but these are not the only bases of privilege and its corollary, prejudice. Later, McIntosh also refers to heterosexual privilege, and her work has influenced the emergence of a series of writings on other ways in which prejudice and privilege manifest themselves in the academy, and ways of addressing these issues.

Similarly, those of us in faculty development who acknowledge that some voices and perspectives are missing have a responsibility to do something about it, beginning with identifying some of the challenges of including missing voices. Because there has been no identifiable single pathway or formal career route into faculty development, entry into the field has often occurred through informal apprenticeship or mentoring. Several of the authors in this volume will attest to having been enticed into the

New Directions for Teaching and Learning • DOI: 10.1002/tl

field in part by the role modeling of a mentor. However, for many of the minority groups whose voices are missing, being mentored is rarely an option. Mentoring relationships often rely on a shared group affiliation or the similar background of mentor and mentee, and because of the under-representation of some groups in the academy there is often little opportu-nity to benefit from such mentoring.

Another challenge is the absence of networks of minority social iden-tity groups, with the possible exception of the HBCU Network mentioned earlier. Networking is a type of political activity that occurs in organiza-tions as a means of developing social relationships that can help individu-als gain access to contacts with valuable information or to decision and policy makers. Successful networks typically depend on a critical mass, but many minorities often experience difficulty in developing such net-works when they are the only one of a specific social identity. This applies not only to individuals but also to entire social identity groups. For exam-ple, intentionally or not, the evolution of faculty development has had a distinctly Western orientation. The philosophy of education that under-pins the work of the present authors has been influenced primarily by scholars from North America, the United Kingdom, Australia, New Zea-land, and to a lesser extent the Scandinavian countries. The International Consortium for Educational Development (ICED), established in 1993 to promote faculty and educational development in postsecondary education throughout the world, has until recently been composed of largely Anglo-phone networks from developed countries. Although there have been recent attempts to include networks from some developing countries, voices from the Caribbean, Latin America, and many regions of Africa are still largely unheard. A complete list of member networks of ICED is avail-able in Lewis's introductory chapter.

Consequences of Exclusion

Exclusion of various unheard voices may reinforce existing approaches to faculty development and replicate current paradigms. It may also limit the extent to which alternative, new perspectives become integrated into the field. Exclusion may also have consequences for different stakeholders. For example, students, faculty, and staff from dominant groups may fail to access opportunities to transform their values, experiences, and beliefs, while the absence of diverse role models in the field may deter those who feel invisible and silenced from entering the field. Some may become alienated, as Darrell McLeod, a Cree, felt about his education in Canada:

> I have spent all of my life living in a dominant society that never validated who I was as an Aboriginal person. My formal education took place in a set-ting where my truths and my world were never reflected in the learning environment. Neither my ways of thinking nor my ways of doing were

validated, even though I believe they were what got me through the system and afforded me whatever success I have experienced. In order to learn what I was being taught, I had to constantly deny the basic tenets of who I am and what I believe (McLeod, 1996, p. 65).

Exclusion may also reduce our capacity to help our institutions achieve their goals of educating for global citizenship. Without modeling multiculturalism and inclusion ourselves, we may lose credibility in the eyes of our various stakeholders. Ultimately, the profession itself is likely to suffer as we lose the richness of perspectives to be gained from diversity. For example, as Scholarship of Teaching and Learning (SoTL) gains momentum, we run the risk of excluding the perspectives of unheard voices from the growing discourse in the many professional journals and conferences now dedicated to SoTL.

Implications

One implication of acknowledging that there are voices missing from the discourse on faculty development is that, as McIntosh (1988) suggests, we must now make it our responsibility to not only identify those unheard voices but also invite, entice, or otherwise actively seek their engagement in the field. Change must occur at the individual, organizational, and community levels.

At the individual level, there is a need for ongoing reflection, learning, and growth. Faculty developers need to ensure that they develop "diversity competence," which refers to "a process of learning that leads to an ability to effectively respond to the challenges and opportunities posed by the presence of socio-cultural diversity in a defined social system" (Cox and Beale, 1997, p. 20). Just as we actively seek to develop competence in an array of skills that we perceive to be relevant and critical to our professional development, so too we need to seek opportunities for increasing our understanding of how the dynamics of diversity affect our institutions, faculty members, and students. The earlier quotation from Darrell McLeod is one example of adverse effects on an individual. More important, we need to be able to change our behavior to take these effects into account. Diversity creates both challenges and opportunities, and competent practitioners are able not only to avoid diversity-related problems but also to tap into the potential of diversity to enhance their own performance and that of others.

Learning diversity competence involves three phases of development: awareness, understanding, and action. The awareness phase is essentially acknowledgment of the need for learning, and recognition that diversity rather than homogeneity pervades our institutions—and that it has the potential to enrich our work. Understanding occurs through acquisition of knowledge, a deeper grasp of how and why diversity competence is relevant to our roles as faculty developers. Increased understanding subsequently leads to action to change the status quo. In the context of our discussion in this chapter, for example, it might entail intentionally seeking out the unheard voices among our constituents and not only giving them a voice but actively heeding them. Among its identifiable benefits, diversity competence enhances communication with others, improves intergroup relations and mutual understanding among people from different cultural groups, and promotes self-discovery and growth. It also increases a commitment to social justice and civic engagement and community service. As McIntosh (1988) argues, we have an individual as well as collective responsibility to examine and reflect on the gaps in our knowledge and social experiences. On the basis of reflection, expanded knowledge, and increased diversity competence, we will be better able to sustain a rich and mutually rewarding dialogue with colleagues whose perspectives may differ from our own. In tandem with institutional and organizational changes, we may usher in an era of transformational teaching and learning for ourselves, our faculty, and ultimately our students.

At the level of the community of faculty developers, our professional associations must work harder to attract diverse voices into their membership, and to put better infrastructure in place to ensure that they are heard. There is an opportunity for STLHE to show leadership in this regard. As a national organization in bilingual Canada, it needs to restructure itself to be more welcoming to its Francophone colleagues. Similarly, our professional associations need to reflect the diversity of institutional types in higher education, including universities, colleges, university colleges, and polytechnics, as well as the diversity of institutions catering to various sociocultural and ethnic groups, such as HBUCs, HSIs, and tribal colleges. Moreover, we need to ensure that these groups are not on the margins of our associations but have a central place in leadership structures where they can be heard. It may therefore be timely to reorient the visions of our professional associations to bring them into closer alignment with socially just issues and enable them to hear previously unheard voices.

Like individual practitioners, the community of faculty developers may need to engage in self-reflection and question whether voices are unheard on account of what we do not do in developing new recruits into the profession. We need to ask ourselves whether our institutions provide sufficient opportunities for graduate students and junior practitioners to develop the capacity to voice their concerns and hear and appreciate different voices. This calls into question our methods of orienting new developers and emphasizes the need for this volume's exploration of pathways into the profession.

Ouellett and Stanley (2004) have suggested that new models for understanding multicultural organizational development must be considered if we are to move forward significantly on reshaping the membership of our field and building an inclusive profession. Schneider (2008) also proposes that we take a careful look at the emerging international body of literature and practices on multicultural education. The current authors' expectation is that we would learn much from these sources. What, for example, might previously unheard voices tell us about how they have learned to teach or practice faculty development? How might they conceptualize communities of practice, a treasured aspect of the professional development of mainstream faculty developers, when many of the unheard voices may belong to faculty developers who practice their work in relative isolation? Where and how do they find their support? Is there a body of literature that exists for their benefit and from which mainstream developers have been excluded? How has the field evolved in parts of the world where philosophies of teaching and faculty development are less collaboratively oriented? What lessons might we learn from the silenced, if we give them opportunities to teach us, and what synergies might be gained by conducting research and practicing faculty development with new lenses that have given us insights into new ways of doing and being? The possibilities may be endless, but we may never know unless we begin to listen to other voices.

References

Cox, Jr. T., and Beale, R. *Developing Competency to Manage Diversity: Readings, Cases and Activities.* San Francisco: Berrett-Koehler, 1997.

Dawkins, P. W., Beach, A. L., and Rozman, S. "Perceptions of Faculty Developers About the Present and Future of Faculty Development at Historically Black Colleges and Universities." *To Improve the Academy,* 2006, *24,* 104–120.

Henry, F., and Tator, C. (eds.). *Searching for Social Justice, Inclusion, and Equity: Racism in the Canadian University.* Toronto, Ont.: University of Toronto Press, 2009.

Johnson, S. M., and Lollar, X. L. "Diversity Policy in Higher Education: The Impact of College Students' Exposure to Diversity on Cultural Awareness and Political Participation." *Journal of Educational Policy,* 2004, *17*(3), 305–320.

McIntosh, P. *White Privilege and Male Privilege: A Personal Account of Coming to See Correspondences Through Work in Women's Studies.* Working Paper 189, Center for Research on Women, Wellesley College, Wellesley, Mass., 1988. Retrieved [February 1, 2010] from http://www.nymbp.org/reference/WhitePrivilege.pdf

McLeod, D. "Instructional Strategies in the Multicultural Classroom." *Community College Journal of Research and Practice,* 1996, *20,* 65–73.

Ouellett, M. L., and Stanley, C. "Fostering Diversity in a Faculty Development Organization." In C. Wehlburg and S. Chadwick-Blossey, *To Improve the Academy.* Bolton, Mass.: Anker, 2004

Schneider, C. G. "Globalization and U.S. Higher Education." *Liberal Education,* 2008, *94*(4), 1–2.

Stanley, C. A. "A Review of the Pipeline: The Value of Diversity in Staffing Teaching and Learning Centers in the New Millennium." *Journal of Faculty Development,* 2001, *18*(2), 75–86.

JOY MIGHTY is director of the Center for Teaching and Learning and a full professor in the School of Business at Queen's University. She is the past president

(2007–2010) of the Society for Teaching and Learning in Higher Education (STLHE), Canada.

MATHEW L. OUELLETT is director of the Center for Teaching and a lecturer in the School of Education at the University of Massachusetts, Amherst. He is a past president (2006–07) of the Professional and Organizational Development (POD) Network in Higher Education, USA.

CHRISTINE A. STANLEY is vice president and associate provost for diversity and a full professor in the College of Education and Human Development at Texas A&M University. She is a past president (2000–01) of the Professional and Organizational Development (POD) Network in Higher Education, USA.

INDEX

Finnish Network for Developing University Teaching (PEDA-forum), 19
Fletcher, J. J., 69, 70, 76
Ford Foundation, 14
Fraser, K., 3, 8, 15, 26, 34, 37–38, 49, 54–56, 86, 94
Frost, S. H., 63
Fund for the Improvement of Postsecondary Education, 16

Gaff, G., 50, 52, 98, 99
Gibbs, G., 19
Ginns, P., 83, 87
Glenn, D., 18
Gosling, D., 3, 4, 8, 15–18, 21, 26, 30, 37–38, 49, 51, 52, 55, 86, 91, 93, 94, 97, 98
Graff, J. G., 13
Grant, B., 93
Gray, K., 84
Great Plains Regional Consortium on Instructional Development, 31
Green, D., 60, 62
Griffith University (Australia), 20

Hannan, A., 17
Hansen, J., 40
Harris, R., 84
Hativa, N., 61
Haynes, A., 70
HBCU Network. See Historically Black Colleges and Universities Faculty Development Network
HELTASA. See Higher Education Learning and Teaching Association of South Africa (HELTASA)
Henkel, M., 100
Henry, F., 105
Hess, S., 40–41
Hicks, M., 93
Hicks, O., 15, 50
Higher Education Funding Council for England, 17, 55
Higher Education Learning and Teaching Association of South Africa (HELTASA), 19, 96
Higher Education Research and Development Society of Australasia (HERDSA), 19, 37
Hill, C., 40–41
Historically Black Colleges and Universities Faculty Development Network

(HBCU Network), 31, 105, 106, 108, 110
Hitchcock, A., 70, 76, 77
Hoessler, C., 4, 8, 81
Holland, J. L., 63
Huber, M. T., 65, 94
Hum, G., 64
Hutchings, P., 52, 65

ICED. See International Consortium for Educational Development (ICED)
Institute for New Faculty Developers (POD Network), 42
International Consortium for Educational Development (ICED), 19–20, 34, 108
Israeli Network of Centers for the Advancement of Teaching in Higher Education (NCATHE), 19

Japan Association for Educational Development in Higher Education (JAED), 19
Jean, P. M., 63
Johnson, S. M., 104
Joint Working Group on Teaching and Learning (OCAV and COED), 75
Justice, D. O., 15

Kahn, P., 37
Kandlbinder, P. A., 7, 93, 94
Kellogg Foundation, 14
Knapper, C., 1, 31, 69
Knight, R. T., 59
Kogan, M., 51
Kolb, D. A., 61
Kotter, J. P., 71–77, 84–86
Kreber, C., 81–84, 87, 100
Kuhn, T. S., 62

Land, R., 38, 50–52, 54, 93, 94, 97
Latin America, 108
Lattuca, L. R., 60, 62
Lave, J., 42
Leading Change (Kotter), 71
Learning and Teaching Subject Centers (United Kingdom), 55
Learning and Teaching Support Network, 16
Lee, A., 7, 37, 93, 94, 101
Lenze, L. F., 83
Leslie, L. L., 100
Lewis, D. R., 50, 54
Lewis, K. G., 3, 7–8, 13, 21, 37, 86, 108
Like, K., 40–41

For a complete list of back issues, please visit www.josseybass.com/go/ndtl

citizens, better equipped to solve complex problems at work and better prepared to lead meaningful lives individually. To respond to this call, teachers in colleges and universities need to learn how to design more powerful kinds of learning into their courses. In 2003, Dee Fink published a seminal book, *Creating Significant Learning Experiences*, that offered teachers two major tools for meeting this need: the Taxonomy of Significant Learning and the model of Integrated Course Design. Since that time, educators around the world have found Fink's ideas both visionary and inspiring. This issue of *New Directions for Teaching and Learning* contains multiple stories of how college-level teachers have used these ideas in a variety of teaching situations, with subject matter ranging from the sciences to the humanities. Their conclusion? The ideas in Fink's book truly make a difference. When used properly, they lead to major improvements in the level of student engagement and the quality of student learning!
ISBN: 978-04705-54807

TL118   **Internationalizing the Curriculum in Higher Education**
Carolin Kreber
Internationalization is a looming policy issue in higher education—yet precisely what it can add to the student learning experience and what it means with regard to teaching and learning are far too infrequently discussed or written about. This volume explores different meanings and rationales underlying the notion of internationalization in higher education. Although internationalization efforts in higher education have become increasingly driven by economic considerations, finance is not an appropriate foundation for all initiatives, particularly those at the level of curriculum, where academic, social/cultural, ethical, political and even environmental rationales feature more strongly. The chapter authors provide a rich conceptual basis from which to appreciate concrete efforts directed at internationalizing curricula, and they describe nine cases of internationalization initiatives at the curricular level. The volume further suggests that consideration of internationalization in higher education must look both within specific programs and across programs. It cannot be separated from fundamental questions about the purposes of higher education and the roles of teachers, students, administrators, and the institution as a whole in fulfilling those purposes.
ISBN: 978-04705-37350

TL117   **Improving the Climate for Undergraduate Teaching and Learning in STEM Fields**
Roger G. Baldwin
The quality of undergraduate education in science, technology, engineering, and mathematics (STEM) fields has been a national concern since the time of Sputnik. In spite of many reports on the state of STEM undergraduate education and multiple reform efforts, time-worn patterns of instruction persist in many STEM classrooms and laboratories. It is increasingly clear that major improvements to STEM under-graduate education require the interest and active engagement of key stakeholders, including STEM instructors, academic administrators, disciplinary societies, and government policy-makers. This volume looks at the challenges of enhancing STEM education from the perspective of these different stakeholders. Each chapter provides an illumi-nating analysis of problems facing STEM education and suggests actions needed to strengthen STEM undergraduate education in a time when science and technology competence are more important than ever. The strategies advanced in this volume should be key elements of the coordinated, systemic effort necessary to implement lasting reform of STEM undergraduate education.
ISBN: 978-04704-97289

TL116 Team-Based Learning: Small-Group Learning's Next Big Step
Larry K. Michaelsen, Michael Sweet, Dean X. Parmelee
Team-Based Learning (TBL) is a unique form of small-group learning designed in and for the college classroom. TBL's special combination of incentives and corrective feedback quickly transforms groups into high-performance learning teams, with no time taken from the coverage of course content. In this issue of *New Directions for Teaching and Learning*, the authors describe the practical elements of TBL, how it can look in the classroom, and what they have learned as it has grown into an inter-disciplinary and international practice. Importantly, TBL is not about teaching but about learning. Several articles in this volume illustrate this emphasis by using TBL students' own words to reinforce key ideas.
ISBN: 978-04704-62126

TL115 The Role of the Classroom in College Student Persistence
John M. Braxton
This issue of *New Directions for Teaching and Learning* brings into sharp focus the complex role college and university faculty play in shaping the persistence and departure decisions of undergraduate students. The authors review practices ranging from curricular structures and instructional staffing policies to faculty teaching methods, and they offer recommendations for many common problems. Taken together, the chapters outline the elements of a scholarship of practice centered on keeping students in school. College and university presidents, chief academic affairs officers, academic deans, directors and staff members of campus-based centers for teaching, and individuals responsible for enrollment management will find a great deal of practical wisdom in this volume.
ISBN: 978-04704-22168

TL114 Information Literacy: One Key to Education
Margit Misangyi Watts
This issue draws on the expertise of librarians and faculty to highlight the central role of information literacy in higher education. The authors show how approaches to information literacy can be used to engage undergrad-uates in research and creative scholarship. The articles clarify definitions of information literacy and illustrate various means of curricular integration. Students regularly miss the relationship between the information-seeking process and the actual creation of knowledge. The authors in this issue support infusing the undergraduate curriculum with research-based learning to facilitate students' ability to define research for themselves. Most impor-tantly, this volume argues, students' information literacy leads beyond find-ing information—it actually involves their creating knowledge. Education should focus on inquiry, research, and discovery as a frame of mind. Our goal as educators should be to maintain and strengthen the *context* of learning while enhancing the *content* of a liberal education. This finally rests—as it always has—on a foundation of incorporating information liter-acy skills. Recent dramatic changes in the meaning of "information literacy" have left many educators scrambling to keep up. What has not changed is the importance of teaching students to find information that matters and then helping them figure out *why* it matters. These chapters can help us all integrate the new world of digital information into a relevant, timely approach to content and teaching practice.
ISBN: 978-04703-98715

TL113 Educating Integrated Professionals: Theory and Practice on Preparation for the Professoriate
Carol L. Colbeck, KerryAnn O'Meara, Ann E. Austin
This volume explores how to enhance doctoral education by preparing future faculty to integrate their work in two interrelated ways. The first

mode encourages doctoral students—and their faculty mentors—to take advantage of the synergies among their teaching, research, and community service roles. The second mode of integration emphasizes connections between professional and academic aspects of faculty work. The authors draw on theories of identity development, professionalization, apprenticeship, socialization, mentoring, social networks, situated curriculum, concurrent curricula, and academic planning to illuminate some of the drawbacks of current education for the professoriate. They also point toward current programs and new possibilities for educating doctoral students who will be ready to begin their faculty careers as professionals who integrate teaching, research, and service.
ISBN: 978-04702-95403

TL112   **Curriculum Development in Higher Education: Faculty-Driven Processes and Practices**
Peter Wolf, Julia Christensen Hughes
Faculty within institutions of higher education are increasingly being asked to play leadership roles in curriculum assessment and reform initiatives.
This change is being driven by quality concerns; burgeoning disciplinary knowledge; interest in a broader array of learning outcomes, including skills and values; and growing support for constructivist pedagogies and learning-centered, interdisciplinary curricula. It is essential that faculty be well prepared to take a scholarly approach to this work. To that end, this issue of *New Directions for Teaching and Learning* presents the frameworks used and lessons learned by faculty, administrators, and educational developers in a variety of curriculum assessment and development processes. Collectively, the authors in this volume present the context and catalysts of higher education curriculum reform, advocate for the Scholarship of Curriculum Practice (SoCP), provide examples of curricular assessment and development initiatives at a variety of institutional levels, suggest that educational developers can provide much support to such processes, and argue that this work has profound implications for the faculty role. Anyone involved in curriculum assessment and development will find food for thought in each chapter.
ISBN: 978-04702-78512

TL111   **Scholarship of Multicultural Teaching and Learning**
Matthew Kaplan, A.T. Miller
Because effective approaches to multicultural teaching and learning are still being developed in institutions across the U.S. and around the world, it is essential to study and document promising practices. It is only through rigorous research and comparative studies that we can be assured that the significant investments many institutions are making in multicultural education for the development of individual student and faculty skills, and the overall betterment of society, will reap positive results. This volume of *New Directions for Teaching and Learning* provides the valuable results of such research as well as models for the types of research that others could carry out in this area. The volume will appeal to new and experienced practitioners of multicultural teaching. It offers documented illustrations of how such teaching is designed, carried out, and is effective in varied higher education contexts and in a wide range of disciplines representing the humanities, social sciences, engineering and math, and the arts.
ISBN: 978-04702-23826

TL110   **Neither White Nor Male: Female Faculty of Color**
Katherine Grace Hendrix
Given limited information on the academic experience in general and on the pedagogical strategies and strengths of faculty of color in particular, the scholars in this issue have come together to begin the process of articulating

the academic experiences of female professors of color. While chronicling our challenges within academia as well as our contributions to the education of U.S. students, this collaborative effort will add depth to the existing literature on faculty of color, serve as a reference for positioning women of color within the larger context of higher education (moving us from the margin to the center), and lay a foundation for more inclusive future research.
ISBN: 04702-2382-6

TL109   **Self-Authorship: Advancing Students' Intellectual Growth**
Peggy S. Meszaros
This issue addresses the limitations of national efforts to focus students' intellectual development narrowly on testing and explores why educators in higher education should consider using the lens of self-authorship and the Learning Partnerships Model for a more holistic model of student intellectual development. The chapters provide examples of institutional transformations needed to support change in teaching and learning and examples of assessment, research, and curricular development based in self-authorship theory. The summary chapter by Marcia Baxter Magolda ties the themes from each of the chapters together and offers promise for the future. The final chapter provides ideas for next steps in promoting the use of self-authorship to advance the intellectual development of college students. The audience for this volume is broad, ranging from college faculty to student affairs faculty and staff to college administrators who are facing assessment challenges for reporting student learning outcomes to their various consti- tuencies, agencies, and boards. This volume should also prove instructive to faculty embarking on curriculum revisions and identifying and measuring student learning outcomes for undergraduate and graduate students.
ISBN: 07879-9721-2

TL108   **Developing Student Expertise and Community: Lessons from How People Learn**
Anthony J. Petrosino, Taylor Martin, Vanessa Svihla
This issue presents research from a collaboration among learning scientists, assessment experts, technologists, and subject-matter experts, with the goal of producing adaptive expertise in students. The model is based on the National Research Council book *How People Learn*. The chapters present case studies of working together to develop learning environments centered on challenge-based instruction. While the strategies and research come from engineering, they are applicable across disciplines to help students think about the process of problem solving.
ISBN: 07879-9574-6

TL107   **Exploring Research-Based Teaching**
Carolin Kreber
Investigates the wide scope research-based teaching, while focusing on two distinct forms. The first sees research-based teaching as student-focused, inquiry-based learning; students become generators of knowledge. The second perspective fixes the lens on teachers; the teaching is characterized by discipline-specific inquiry into the teaching process itself. Both methods have positive effects on student learning, and this volume explores research and case studies.
ISBN: 07879-9077-9

TL106   **Supplemental Instruction: New Visions for Empowering Student Learning**
Marion E. Stone, Glen Jacobs
Supplemental Instruction (SI) is an academic support model introduced over thirty years ago to help students be successful in difficult courses. SI teaches students how to learn via regularly scheduled, out-of-class collaborative

sessions with other students. This volume both introduces the tenets of SI to beginners and brings those familiar up to speed with today's methods and the future directions. Includes case studies, how-to's, benefits to students and faculty, and more.
ISBN: 0-7879-8680-1

TL105   **A Laboratory for Public Scholarship and Democracy**
Rosa A. Eberly, Jeremy Cohen
Public scholarship has grown out of the scholarship-and-service model, but its end is democracy rather than volunteerism. The academy has intellectual and creative resources that can help build involved, democratic communities through public scholarship. Chapters present concepts, processes, and case studies from Penn State's experience with public scholarship.
ISBN: 0-7879-8530-9

TL104   **Spirituality in Higher Education**
Sherry L. Hoppe, Bruce W. Speck
With chapters by faculty and administrators, this book investigates the role of spirituality in educating the whole student while recognizing that how spirituality is viewed, taught, and experienced is intensely personal. The goal is not to prescribe a method for integrating spirituality but to offer options and perspectives. Readers will be reminded that the quest for truth and meaning, not the destination, is what is vitally important.
ISBN: 0-7879-8363-2

TL103   **Identity, Learning, and the Liberal Arts**
Ned Scott Laff
Argues that we must foster conversations between liberal studies and student development theory, because the skills inherent in liberal learning are the same skills used for personal development. Students need to experience core learning that truly influences their critical thinking skills, character development, and ethics. Educators need to design student learning encounters that develop these areas. This volume gives examples of how liberal arts education can be a healthy foundation for life skills.
ISBN: 0-7879-8333-0

TL102   **Advancing Faculty Learning Through Interdisciplinary Collaboration**
Elizabeth G. Creamer, Lisa R. Lattuca
Explores why stakeholders in higher education should refocus attention on collaboration as a form of faculty learning. Chapters give theoretical basis then practical case studies for collaboration's benefits in outreach, scholarship, and teaching. Also discusses impacts on education policy, faculty hiring and development, and assessment of collaborative work.
ISBN: 0-7879-8070-6

TL101   **Enhancing Learning with Laptops in the Classroom**
Linda B. Nilson, Barbara E. Weaver
This volume contains case studies—mostly from Clemson University's leading-edge laptop program—that address victories as well as glitches in teaching with laptop computers in the classroom. Disciplines using laptops include psychology, music, statistics, animal sciences, and humanities. The volume also advises faculty on making a laptop mandate successful at their university, with practical guidance for both pedagogy and student learning.
ISBN: 0-7879-8049-8

TL100   **Alternative Strategies for Evaluating Student Learning**
Michelle V. Achacoso, Marilla D. Svinicki
Teaching methods are adapting to the modern era, but innovation in assessment of student learning lags behind. This volume examines

theory and practical examples of creative new methods of evaluation, including authentic testing, testing with multimedia, portfolios, group exams, visual synthesis, and performance-based testing. Also investigates improving students' ability to take and learn from tests, before and after.
ISBN: 0-7879-7970-8

TL99   **Addressing Faculty and Student Classroom Improprieties**
John M. Braxton, Alan E. Bayer
Covers the results of a large research study on occurrence and perceptions of classroom improprieties by both students and faculty. When classroom norms are violated, all parties in a classroom are affected, and teaching and learning suffer. The authors offer guidelines for both student and faculty classroom behavior and how institutions might implement those suggestions.
ISBN: 0-7879-7794-2

TL98   **Decoding the Disciplines: Helping Students Learn Disciplinary Ways of Thinking**
David Pace, Joan Middendorf
The Decoding the Disciplines model is a way to teach students the critical-thinking skills required to understand their specific discipline. Faculty define bottlenecks to learning, dissect the ways experts deal with the problematic issues, and invent ways to model experts' thinking for students. Chapters are written by faculty in diverse fields who successfully used these methods and became involved in the scholarship of teaching and learning.
ISBN: 0-7879-7789-6

TL97   **Building Faculty Learning Communities**
Milton D. Cox, Laurie Richlin
A very effective way to address institutional challenges is a faculty learning community. FLCs are useful for preparing future faculty, reinvigorating senior faculty, and implementing new courses, curricula, or campus initiatives. The results of FLCs parallel those of student learning communities, such as retention, deeper learning, respect for others, and greater civic participation. This volume describes FLCs from a practitioner's perspective, with plenty of advice, wisdom, and lessons for starting your own FLC.
ISBN: 0-7879-7568-0

TL96   **Online Student Ratings of Instruction**
Trav D. Johnson, D. Lynn Sorenson
Many institutions are adopting Web-based student ratings of instruction, or are considering doing it, because online systems have the potential to save time and money among other benefits. But they also present a number of challenges. The authors of this volume have firsthand experience with electronic ratings of instruction. They identify the advantages, consider costs and benefits, explain their solutions, and provide recommendations on how to facilitate online ratings.
ISBN: 0-7879-7262-2

TL95   **Problem-Based Learning in the Information Age**
Dave S. Knowlton, David C. Sharp
Provides information about theories and practices associated with problem-based learning, a pedagogy that allows students to become more engaged in their own education by actively interpreting information. Today's professors are adopting problem-based learning across all disciplines to faciliate a broader, modern definition of what it means to learn. Authors provide practical experience about designing useful problems, creating conducive learning environments, facilitating students' activities, and assessing students' efforts at problem solving.
ISBN: 0-7879-7172-3

TL94 Technology: Taking the Distance out of Learning
Margit Misangyi Watts
This volume addresses the possibilities and challenges of computer
technology in higher education. The contributors examine the pressures to
use technology, the reasons not to, the benefits of it, the feeling of being a
learner as well as a teacher, the role of distance education, and the place of
computers in the modern world. Rather than discussing only specific
successes or failures, this issue addresses computers as a new cultural
symbol and begins meaningful conversations about technology in general
and how it affects education in particular.
ISBN: 0-7879-6989-3

TL93 Valuing and Supporting Undergraduate Research
Joyce Kinkead
The authors gathered in this volume share a deep belief in the value of
undergraduate research. Research helps students develop skills in problem
solving, critical thinking, and communication, and undergraduate
researchers' work can contribute to an institution's quest to further
knowledge and help meet societal challenges. Chapters provide an overview
of undergraduate research, explore programs at different types of
institutions, and offer suggestions on how faculty members can find ways to
work with undergraduate researchers.
ISBN: 0-7879-6907-9

TL92 The Importance of Physical Space in Creating Supportive Learning
Environments
Nancy Van Note Chism, Deborah J. Bickford
The lack of extensive dialogue on the importance of learning spaces in
higher education environments prompted the essays in this volume. Chapter
authors look at the topic of learning spaces from a variety of perspectives,
elaborating on the relationship between physical space and learning, arguing
for an expanded notion of the concept of learning spaces and furnishings,
talking about the context within which decision making for learning spaces
takes place, and discussing promising approaches to the renovation of old
learning spaces and the construction of new ones.
ISBN: 0-7879-6344-5

TL91 Assessment Strategies for the On-Line Class: From Theory to Practice
Rebecca S. Anderson, John F. Bauer, Bruce W. Speck
Addresses the kinds of questions that instructors need to ask themselves as
they begin to move at least part of their students' work to an on-line format.
Presents an initial overview of the need for evaluating students' on-line work
with the same care that instructors give to the work in hard-copy format.
Helps guide instructors who are considering using on-line learning in
conjunction with their regular classes, as well as those interested in going
totally on-line.
ISBN: 0-7879-6343-7

TL90 Scholarship in the Postmodern Era: New Venues, New Values, New
Visions
Kenneth J. Zahorski
A little over a decade ago, Ernest Boyer's *Scholarship Reconsidered* burst upon
the academic scene, igniting a robust national conversation that maintains
its vitality to this day. This volume aims at advancing that important
conversation. Its first section focuses on the new settings and circumstances
in which the act of scholarship is being played out; its second identifies and
explores the fresh set of values currently informing today's scholarly
practices; and its third looks to the future of scholarship, identifying trends,

causative factors, and potentialities that promise to shape scholars and their scholarship in the new millennium.
ISBN: 0-7879-6293-7

TL89   **Applying the Science of Learning to University Teaching and Beyond**
Diane F. Halpern, Milton D. Hakel
Seeks to build on empirically validated learning activities to enhance what and how much is learned and how well and how long it is remembered. Demon-strates that the movement for a real science of learning—the application of scientific principles to the study of learning—has taken hold both under the controlled conditions of the laboratory and in the messy real-world settings where most of us go about the business of teaching and learning.
ISBN: 0-7879-5791-7

TL88   **Fresh Approaches to the Evaluation of Teaching**
Christopher Knapper, Patricia Cranton
Describes a number of alternative approaches, including interpretive and critical evaluation, use of teaching portfolios and teaching awards, performance indicators and learning outcomes, technology-mediated evaluation systems, and the role of teacher accreditation and teaching scholarship in instructional evaluation.
ISBN: 0-7879-5789-5

TL87   **Techniques and Strategies for Interpreting Student Evaluations**
Karron G. Lewis
Focuses on all phases of the student rating process—from data-gathering methods to presentation of results. Topics include methods of encouraging meaningful evaluations, mid-semester feedback, uses of quality teams and focus groups, and creating questions that target individual faculty needs and interest.
ISBN: 0-7879-5789-5

TL86   **Scholarship Revisited: Perspectives on the Scholarship of Teaching**
Carolin Kreber
Presents the outcomes of a Delphi Study conducted by an international panel of academics working in faculty evaluation scholarship and postsecondary teaching and learning. Identifies the important components of scholarship of teaching, defines its characteristics and outcomes, and explores its most pressing issues.
ISBN: 0-7879-5447-0

TL85   **Beyond Teaching to Mentoring**
Alice G. Reinarz, Eric R. White
Offers guidelines to optimizing student learning through classroom activities as well as peer, faculty, and professional mentoring. Addresses mentoring techniques in technical training, undergraduate business, science, and liberal arts studies, health professions, international study, and interdisciplinary work.
ISBN: 0-7879-5617-1

NEW DIRECTIONS FOR TEACHING AND LEARNING

ORDER FORM SUBSCRIPTION AND SINGLE ISSUES

DISCOUNTED BACK ISSUES:

Use this form to receive 20% off all back issues of *New Directions for Teaching and Learning*.
All single issues priced at **$23.20** (normally $29.00)

TITLE	ISSUE NO.	ISBN
_____	_____	_____
_____	_____	_____
_____	_____	_____

*Call 888-378-2537 or see mailing instructions below. When calling, mention the promotional code JBXND
to receive your discount. For a complete list of issues, please visit www.josseybass.com/go/ndtl*

SUBSCRIPTIONS: (1 YEAR, 4 ISSUES)

☐ New Order   ☐ Renewal

U.S.	☐ Individual: $89	☐ Institutional: $242
CANADA/MEXICO	☐ Individual: $89	☐ Institutional: $282
ALL OTHERS	☐ Individual: $113	☐ Institutional: $316

*Call 888-378-2537 or see mailing and pricing instructions below.
Online subscriptions are available at www.interscience.wiley.com*

ORDER TOTALS:

Issue / Subscription Amount: $ _____

Shipping Amount: $ _____
(for single issues only – subscription prices include shipping)

Total Amount: $ _____

SHIPPING CHARGES:		
SURFACE	**DOMESTIC**	**CANADIAN**
First Item	$5.00	$6.00
Each Add'l Item	$3.00	$1.50

*(No sales tax for U.S. subscriptions. Canadian residents, add GST for subscription orders. Individual rate subscriptions must
be paid by personal check or credit card. Individual rate subscriptions may not be resold as library copies.)*

BILLING & SHIPPING INFORMATION:

☐ **PAYMENT ENCLOSED:** *(U.S. check or money order only. All payments must be in U.S. dollars.)*

☐ **CREDIT CARD:** ☐ VISA ☐ MC ☐ AMEX

Card number _____ Exp. Date _____

Card Holder Name _____ Card Issue # *(required)* _____

Signature _____ Day Phone _____

☐ **BILL ME:** *(U.S. institutional orders only. Purchase order required.)*

Purchase order # _____
Federal Tax ID 13559302 • GST 89102-8052

Name _____

Address _____

Phone _____ E-mail _____

Copy or detach page and send to: **John Wiley & Sons, PTSC, 5th Floor**
989 Market Street, San Francisco, CA 94103-1741

Order Form can also be faxed to: **888-481-2665**

PROMO JBXND